D0765295

Brain Power Through Picture Books

Brain Power
Through
Picture Books

Help Children Develop
with Books That Stimulate
Specific Parts of Their Minds

by
Nancy J. Polette

McFarland & Company, Inc., Publishers
Jefferson, North Carolina, and London

Acknowledgments: Illustrations on pages 2 and 4 by Paul Dillon; reprinted with the permission of Book Lures, Inc. Whole Brain Model by Ned Herrmann, page 3, reproduced with permission of Dr. Ned Herrmann from *The Creative Brain;* ©1989. Applied Creative Services. Original illustrations by Jodi Barklage on pages 8, 10, 15, 16, 48, 56, 57, 58, 59, 61, 62, 74 reprinted with permission from *Concert Reading;* ©1989. Book Lures, Inc. Lifetime Knowledge Graph, page 11, and Figure 3.1, page 28, reprinted with the permission of Dr. Foster Cline, M.D., from *What Shall We Do with This Kid?* Evergreen, CO, 1979. Illustrations and activities on pages 5, 7, 17, 32, 47, 60, 85, 86, 87, 88 reprinted with permission from *The ABCs of Thinking with Caldecott Books* by Edythe Bernhardt; ©1989 Book Lures, Inc.

Jacket illustrations are included with the permission of the publishers of the books for:

Carle, Eric. *The Very Busy Spider.* Philomel reissue, 1989.
Ventura, Piero. *Michelangelo's World.* Philomel, 1989.
Cole, Babette. *Three Cheers for Errol!* Putnam's, 1989.
Cole, Babette. *King Change-a-Lot.* Putnam's, 1989.
Brown, Marcia. *Once a Mouse.* Scribner's, 1961.
Hogrogian, Nonny. *One Fine Day.* Macmillan, 1971.
McDermott, Gerald. *Arrow to the Sun.* Viking, 1974.
Ward, Lynd. *The Biggest Bear.* Houghton Mifflin, 1951.
Hader, Elmer and Berta. *The Big Snow.* Macmillan, 1948.
Hodges, Margaret. *St. George and the Dragon.* Little, Brown, 1984.

British Library Cataloguing-in-Publication data are available

Library of Congress Cataloguing-in-Publication Data

Polette, Nancy J.
    Brain power through picture books : help children develop with
books that stimulate specific parts of their minds / by Nancy J.
Polette.
        p.   cm.
    Includes bibliographical references and index.
    ISBN 0-89950-708-5 (sewn softcover : 55# alk. paper) ∞
    1. Thought and thinking—Study and teaching (Elementary)
2. Cognition in children.   3. Learning.   4. Children—Books and
reading.   I. Title.
LB1590.3.P65   1992
372'.01'9—dc20   91-50976
                                                      CIP

McFarland & Company, Inc., Publishers
  Box 611, Jefferson, North Carolina 28640

Table of Contents

1

Exercising the Brain: Research Into Action

This book is about brain power and literacy and how children can be helped to live fuller, richer lives through early and constant exposure to books selected specifically to stimluate each part of the growing, developing mind. In her book *Your Child's Growing Mind* (Doubleday, 1987), Dr. Jane Healy brings together the work of many researchers to explain that during the early years neural networks grow in the child's brain as a result of the mental and physical activities of the child. Every time the child responds to new sights, sounds, smells, tastes or touches actual new physical connections are formed in the brain. Consequently, the more neural networks or connections one has, the greater his or her mental powers and abilities will be.

Knowledge of brain development combined with the research of Dr. Ned Herrmann on the four very different thinking modes of the brain provides exciting possibilities for those who parent or teach young children. If exercising each of the four thinking modes can stimulate brain development then parents and teachers alike must be aware of the many possibilities of using literature to help children develop to their fullest potential.

The deliberate selection of specific types of books can stimulate different areas of the brain causing growth of neural networks. The parent who helps his or her child to start a love affair with books for life is at the same time taking a giant step toward assuring the full mental development of the child.

Beautiful, meaningful, delightful and even hilarious rewards await those who are tuned in and not turned off to the reading experience. Children who are allowed to sample with a parent a rich background of literature and encouraged to explore and uncover new treasures for themselves do flourish. Parents, too, have a lifetime of growth ahead of them through sharing the joy and warmth of good literature with their children. The child who has been exposed to the unending supply of ideas and sustenance through

1

contact with books is assured of continual regenerating education. Great minds of the present and past have left their inspiration for all to sample and imbibe from the printed page. How tragic to think that any child, man or woman on this earth might not be exposed to the wisdom, wit and inspiration of the ages.

What a glorious lot is that of the parent today! To bring the young and the great together. Books that are worth reading at all (and many of the great writers of all time have written for children) are bursting with experiences that will touch and stimulate growth in each part of the young child's brain. Love, hate, fear, superstition, remorse, compassion and tenderness come to life under the pen of an inspired writer. Great works of art bring forth responses in all of us as they touch our deepest instincts. Eternal values lurk within every great and good book, even if it is only the necessity for laughter and delight in our lives. A parent cannot always know precisely when the child is ready for a particular concept in a certain book which will burst into his mind with a new light and understanding and illuminate things he has ever known. Hence the necessity for sharing a vast variety of types of books.

The types of books suggested in this book are not randomly selected. They are specifically chosen to stimulate mental activity in all four quadrants of the child's brain and to develop those thinking processes essential to successful living and learning.

Much of popular psychology today would label human beings as "right-brained" or "left-brained." However, the work of many 20th century psychologists including Anthony Gregorc, Berniece McCarthy and Ned Herrmann indicates that the two part model is too simplistic. Most researchers today agree that the four quadrants of the brain control specific thinking processes. This model is easily understood and has far reaching implications for you as a parent in understanding the personal uniqueness of your child and in helping your child to develop a wide variety of skills and abilities. The following model is by Ned Herrmann:

WHOLE BRAIN MODEL

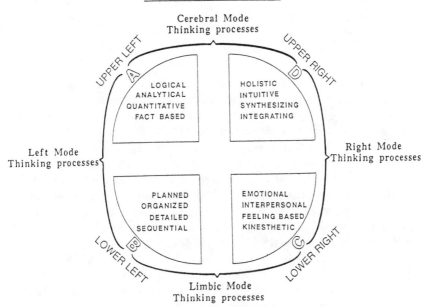

The idea of whole brain development is based on the fact that the brain can be divided horizontally as well as vertically, with each quadrant having specialized functions.

The upper left (thinker) quadrant controls logical, analytical thought. A person with an over-abundance of neural connections in this quadrant is very good at memorizing, analyzing and retaining information. These, of

THINKING PROCESSES OF THE FOUR QUADRANTS

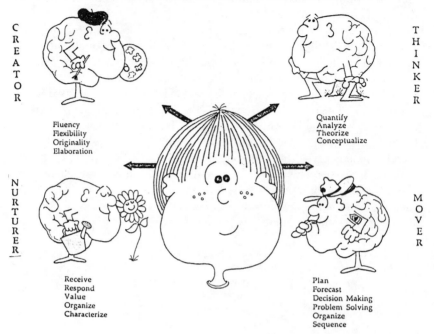

C
R
E
A
T
O
R

Fluency
Flexibility
Originality
Elaboration

T
H
I
N
K
E
R

Quantify
Analyze
Theorize
Conceptualize

N
U
R
T
U
R
E
R

Receive
Respond
Value
Organize
Characterize

M
O
V
E
R

Plan
Forecast
Decision Making
Problem Solving
Organize
Sequence

course, are qualities valued in school and these children often score high on tests and are frequently identified for gifted programs. The kinds of books to share with young children to stimulate neural growth in this quadrant are those that deal with reality and life itself . . . books that can reawaken or confirm that awe and mystery surrounding all living things. A sense of wonder and an appreciation of beauty . . . whether of a grass blade or a star . . . are inherent with children, and books can nourish this. Books dealing with reality can help the child to listen more acutely, look more intently, feel more sensitively, taste more discerningly and touch more genuinely the astonishing world of reality surrounding us all. We begin with real or fact-based material which stimulates growth in the upper left quadrant, but by carefully selecting that material we can touch also the quadrants of the brain that deal with organization, feeling and creativity.

Among the excellent picture books that present the real world in all its wonder are many titles by Seymour Simon, Millicent Selsam, Franklyn Branley, Lawrence Pringle and a host of other writers.

The development of a strong working vocabulary is another function of the left side of the brain. The emphasis on language development is in the upper left quadrant but both upper and lower left quadrants are involved. It is true that in order to control one's thinking, language must be simplified. This is certainly one of the reasons totalitarian governments burn books.

LOGIC PUZZLE

ONE-EYE, TWO-EYES, AND THREE-EYES

Three sisters each had three eyes. They each had two eyes like other people and one additional eye. One had her extra eye on a finger, one had hers on a toe, and one had hers on the top of her head. Their names were Sara, Tara, and Mim.

They each also had an unusual pet dog. One dog had two tails, one had six legs, and one had wings. One girl ate only fruit, another ate only vegetables, and a third ate only meat.

Use the clues below to find answers to the following questions:

Who had her extra eye on her finger?_____
Whose dog had six legs?_____
Who ate only meat? _____

Sara found her extra eye was valuable when she was reaching into the tree to get her food.

Tara could see her dog above her without tipping her head.

Carrots were Mim's favorite food.

The place where each girl had an extra eye never started with the same letter as the extra body part of her dog.

	HEAD	FINGER	TOE	TAILS	WINGS	LEGS	FRUIT	VEGETABLES	MEAT
SARA									
TARA									
MIM									

Conversely, to expand the ability to think we must expand the child's language storehouse . . . those words he or she carries in the brain to speak and write with ease.

Language patterns get to the brain through the ear. From 10 to 20 exposures are usually needed before a pattern goes into the long term memory

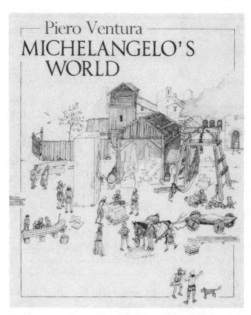

and can be used. Words are the tools of our thoughts and experience. All of us respond to the sound of language, the flow of words, the variety of tones and combinations of signals. Many creators of picture books revel in our language, its cadences and intricacies. We can join in their fun of playing with words and help the child's ear to delight in the richness of language by sharing aloud many fine books including the *Just So Stories* of Rudyard Kipling, *Mother Goose*, and the books of Beatrix Potter, Lewis Carroll and A.A. Milne.

The lower left quadrant (mover) deals with the efficient use of information. It allows one to plan, organize, sequence information, problem-solve and work with details. It is interesting to note that nearly every major psychologist states that the basic key to intellectual growth is the ability to see patterns and relationships. Neural stimulation in this lower left quadrant helps to build this ability. Among many fine picture books that deal with sequencing, grouping, patterns and relationships are Pat Hutchins's *Changes, Changes*, Pamela Allen's *Bertie and the Bear*, Niki Yektai's *Bears in Pairs*, Elizabeth Winthrop's *Shoes*, Eric Carle's *Very Busy Spider* and Susan Hellard's *This Little Piggy*. Delightful problem-solving situations arise in Pat McKissack's *Flossie and the Fox* and *Mirandy and Brother Wind*.

Other titles which stimulate contextual thinking include Pamela Allen's *Hidden Treasure*, Catherine Brighton's *Five Secrets in a Box*, Donald Carrick's *Harald and the Giant Knight*, Joanna Cole's *Magic School Bus Goes to the Waterworks*, Steven Manes's *Life Is No Fair*, James Marshall's *George and Martha* series, Tony Ross's *The Boy Who Cried Wolf*, Marcia Vaughan's

DECISION MAKING

Lower Left Quadrant
Activity

HOME SWEET HOME

Help Mr. and Mrs. Mallard decide
where to live and raise their family.

1. Choose three places ducks could live in your community.
2. Check to see if these places have things ducks need.
3. Where would you choose to live if you were a duck?

Score: Yes or No	Peace and Quiet	Plenty of Good Food	Source of Water	Safety from Enemies

(left axis label: Places Ducks Could Live)

Make Way for Ducklings by Robert McCloskey, Viking Press, 1941.

Wombat Stew, Barbara Williams's *Albert's Toothache* and Don and Audrey Woods's *Heckedy Peg.*

The lower right quadrant of the brain (*The Nurturer*) controls emotions, feelings, relationships and kinesthetic ability. The person with strength in this quadrant (ample neural connections) can be very empathetic, usually works well with other people and enjoys music, sports and good

food. Since this is the feeling-based quadrant, the child who has had many
early childhood experiences in a "warm fuzzy" family is very likely to
develop into a warm, nurturing person. In such a family the lower right
quadrant is stimulated again and again causing more neural connections to
form here. Surely one of the greatest needs in the world today is that of

resolving human relationships peacefully. Nations find it hard to understand one another, as do their inhabitants. Books about people facing real challenges, having real feelings can help children to understand and empathize with our common problems and fears. Books which can evoke sincere feeling (as television rarely is able to do) are essential in the literary diet. Such books can bless and benefit the child and ultimately all others who may be touched by his or her life.

There are literally hundreds of choices of books which will stimulate growth in this lower right quadrant, books that touch the heart. Cecil Alexander's *All Things Bright and Beautiful* and Babette Cole's *Three Cheers for Errol!* stimulate feelings of awe and joy. Parent and child will indeed have a warm delightful story time with any of the *Frog and Toad* books by Arnold Lobel. The caring friendship of these two famous literary characters will help your child to become a more loving, caring adult. For those who claim that books are vicarious experiences, not real life, one must note that the tears shed by the reader/listener to Rebecca Caudill's *A Certain Small Shepherd* are very real indeed!

Finally, the upper right quadrant of the brain (the creator) deals with visual, creative, intuitive abilities which allow one to see things in new ways and to create new ideas, new products and new ways of doing things. The creator is impulsive, likes change and risk and has little use for time. More importantly, the creator is aware of beauty in his or her surroundings and

CREATIVE THINKING

can create beauty for others. Imagination and fantasy are abilities of the upper right quadrant and are vital ingredients to a full and rich life. They poke fun at reality, play with it, brighten it and eventually illumine it. The daily routing of required pursuits tends to squelch the creative brain. The right books can keep it nurtured and alive. Fantasy need not be heavy or ponderous.

Babette Cole's *Princess Smartypants* and *King Change-a-lot* as well as Anno's *Topsy Turvies* are often simmering with chuckles and surprises. The sharing of imaginative literature can stimulate growth in this upper right quadrant.

Obviously we all have whole brains and are capable of the thinking processes located in each of the four quadrants. However, Ned Herrman's studies indicate that the majority of people show strength in one or two quadrants and that of the nearly one half million people he has tested, only five percent show equal strength in all four quadrants.

According to Dr. Foster Cline, 75 to 80 percent of the child's brain development takes place before the child enters school. Through providing a wide variety of activities that stimulate neurological development in each of the four quadrants, young children can be helped to achieve greater brain power.

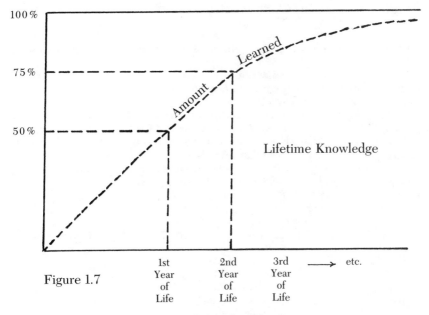

Figure 1.7

Learning Takes Place
Along a
Logarithmic Curve

At the end of the first year of life, we have an organism of extreme sophistication. Think of the joy that a computer designer would feel if he could design a "thing" that could attend to sound, track it, organize it, go over to it, pick it up. — *What Shall We Do with This Kid* by Foster W. Cline, M.D. 1979 (P.O. Box 14, Evergreen, CO 80439).

Help is what *Brain Power Through Picture Books* is intended to be — help with selecting books to stimulate thinking in the intellectual, contextual, affective and creative realms, help with the selection of the finest books available in children's literature and help in building warm adult-child relationships through the sharing of books, yardsticks upon which the child will unconsciously measure what is worthy against what is trivial.

References

Cline, Foster. *What Shall We Do with This Kid.* Evergreen, CO, 1979.
Healy, Jane. *Your Child's Growing Mind.* Doubleday, 1987.
Herrmann, Ned. *The Creative Brain.* Applied Creative Services, 2075 Buffalo Creek Road, Lake Lure, NC 28746.
Polette, Nancy and Hamlin, Marjorie. *E Is for Everybody.* Scarecrow Press, 1975.

Suggested Children's Reading

Alexander, Cecil. *All Things Bright and Beautiful.* Grossett and Dunlap, 1989.
Allen, Pamela. *Bertie and the Bear.* Putnam's, 1985; *The Hidden Treasure.* Putnam's, 1987.
Anno, Mitsumasa. *Topsy Turvies.* Putnam reissue, 1989.
Brighton, Catherine. *Five Secrets in a Box.* Dutton, 1987.
Carle, Eric. *Very Busy Spider.* Philomel reissue, 1989.
Carrick, Donald. *Harald and the Giant Knight.* Clarion, 1982.
Caudill, Rebecca. *A Certain Small Shepherd.* Holt, 1965.
Cole, Babette. *King Change-a-lot.* Putnam's, 1989; *Princess Smartypants.* Putnam's, 1987; *Three Cheers for Errol!* Putnam's, 1989.
Cole, Joanna. *Magic School Bus at the Waterworks.* Doubleday, 1986.
Fjuikawa, Gyo. *Mother Goose.* Grosset and Dunlap, 1987.
Hellard, Susan. *This Little Piggy.* Philomel, 1989.
Hutchins, Pat. *Changes, Changes.* Macmillan, 1971.
Lobel, Arnold. *Days with Frog and Toad.* Harper and Row, 1979.
McKissack, Patricia. *Flossie and the Fox.* Dial, 1987; *Mirandy and Brother Wind.* Knopf, 1988.
Manes, Steven. *Life Is No Fair.* Coward-McCann, 1986.
Ross, Tony. *The Boy Who Cried Wolf.* Dial, 1987.
Tejima. *Woodpecker Forest.* Philomel, 1989.
Vaughan, Marcia. *Wombat Stew.* Simon Shuster, 1986.
Ventura, Piero. *Michelangelo's World.* Philomel, 1989.
Williams, Barbara. *Albert's Toothache.* Dutton, 1974.
Winthrop, Elizabeth. *Shoes.* Harper and Row, 1986.
Yektai, Niki. *Bears in Pairs.* Four Winds, 1988.

2

Developing Early
Childhood Thinking Skills

Gina's parents had read aloud to her from the cradle, sharing the richest treasures of literature from *Mother Goose* to *Winnie the Pooh*. When Gina entered school she had over 20,000 language patterns in her head, patterns essential to successful reading. Gina was a bright child, highly verbal, creative and outgoing. Everything pointed to her success in school, yet Gina did not read. Her frantic parents conferred with the teacher who assured them that Gina was indeed a bright child and that forcing reading before Gina was ready could result in stress, anxiety, frustration and possible long term damage. The teacher urged Gina's parents to relax and to continue reading aloud. How fast Gina would move academically was not the question. How far she would eventually go was of more importance.

Gina began reading in grade two and like Robert Kraus's hero, Leo, the Late Bloomer, she did not stumble over individual words but read fluently, easily and with a high level of understanding. By grade three Gina's parents were faced with another problem . . . how to get her to stop reading long enough to do other things.

The renowned Swiss psychologist, Jean Piaget, theorized that many thinking tasks depend on the child's developmental time table and that all children are not ready for particular mental tasks at the same time. Some children, for example, read fluently at age four, others not until age eight and as Piaget discovered, early reading and exceptional intellectual ability did not necessarily go together.

Current brain research tells us that Piaget was right. Readiness for many intellectual tasks including the ability to read depends on the maturation of neuron systems, particularly the full development of the prefrontal lobes of the brain. This development takes place somewhere between the ages of four and eight. Thus, trying to speed reading or to force learning over incomplete neuron systems is the same as expecting a child who has never had a piano lesson to play a Mozart concerto!

13

What Are the Intellectual Tasks of Early Childhood?

Important to academic success are four intellectual tasks as defined by Piaget.

Conservation: Recognizing that an object does not lose mass if you change its shape and or that a set number of objects remain the same no matter how the objects are grouped. A simple test for conservation is to take two balls of clay of exactly the same size. Ask the young child which has more clay. Hopefully the child will recognize the balls as being the same. Now take one of the balls and roll it into a long snake. Then ask the child which has more clay. The child who cannot conserve will identify the snake as having more clay. This child should not begin formal reading.

Are the boys in the picture (opposite page) two different boys or is this the same boy? How can you tell?

Seriation: Recognizing the order of things. One to ten, A to Z, largest to smallest, etc. *The ability to identify sequence.*

ABOUT THE BOOK: In Marcia Brown's book, *Once a Mouse,* an older hermit, mighty at magic, made a tiger from a mouse. The hermit befriended a frightened little mouse. When a cat attempted to attack the mouse, the hermit turned the little mouse into a stout cat, then into a big dog and finally into a proud and royal tiger. The hermit reminded the proud tiger of his humble beginnings which angered the tiger who plotted against the hermit. Being magic, the hermit could read the tiger's mind and put the proud tiger in his place — as a frightened, humble, little mouse. And the hermit sat thinking about big — and little.

SHARING QUESTIONS:
1. What happened first in the story? What happened next? Last?
2. Can you name all the animals in the story from smallest to largest?

Classification: The ability to group within categories. Young children tend to identify objects in a group by function ("You eat with these," "You play with these"). As neuron systems mature, the child will begin to group by quality, hard things, things with corners, etc.

Reversibility: Recognizing reverse operations, following a line of thought back to its beginning. This is an essential skill for mathematics as well as reading.

ABOUT THE BOOK: *One Fine Day* is a story by Nonny Hogrogian which tells of a greedy fox who steals an old woman's milk. The old woman angrily cuts off the tail of the fox. The fox is ashamed before his freinds and asks her to sew his tail on again. But the old woman will not sew on his tail unless the fox brings her milk from the cow. When the fox asks the cow for milk for the old woman, the cow demands some grass for the milk. The fox visits

Les, the Mess

A boy named Les
Was such a mess.
His stringy hair
Was everywhere.
And then one day his mom was firm,
Gave Les a curly, girly perm!

How many groups of things can you find in this picture. (A group must be more than two.)

a field for some grass only to have the field ask for some water in return for the grass. And so the story goes on and on, until the fox completes all the requests and can return with the milk for the old woman. The old woman then carefully sews the tail of the fox back on again.

The Bunny and Farmer Brown's Carrots

One sunny day, a bunny was hungry and wanted to go eat carrots at Farmer Brown's garden.

On the way, the bunny stopped to smell the flowers. Then he hopped on down the path to a big tree.

After he rested awhile, the bunny saw a turtle and wanted to play. But the turtle wanted to sleep, so the bunny hopped on to the garden.

The bunny saw a leaf on the path and wanted to eat it. When a worm crawled from under the leaf, the bunny hopped down the path.

Bunny wanted to eat a carrot more than he wanted to eat a worm. Bunny found Farmer Brown's garden and ate until he was full. He wanted to go back home to take a nap.

REVERSIBLE THINKING

Can you help Bunny hop back home?

It is important to note that until the child is ready these skills cannot be taught. They can be taught, however, when the child's neurological systems are sufficiently mature. What can parents do? Since it is difficult to determine that precise moment of readiness, parents can, beginning when the child is very young . . . share those mind-stretching picture books which touch upon these four processes. A good story and a loving parent provide invaluable experiences for the child. If your child seems eager you can extend the experience by asking questions that arise naturally from the text.

Master teacher Connie Cozzoni provides a model for the kinds of questions that will stimulate brain growth and new ways of thinking.

When sharing Eric Carle's *1, 2, 3, to the Zoo* (Collins-World, 1968) use this type of questioning: What animal do you see in the first car? How many elephants are there? What do you see in the second car? How many? Before I turn the page, how many animals do you think there will be in the next car? Why do you think it will be three? On the last page there are no animals on the train. Where are they? How do you know these are the same animals? Let's make sure. On the first car there was one _____? Find that elephant in the zoo.

Before sharing Tana Hoban's *Circles, Triangles and Squares* (Greenwillow, 1984) make hand circles in the air. Find something in the room that is the shape of a circle. How many sides does the triangle have? On each page find the different shapes in the picture. Ask, "If I turn the book upside down will it still be a triangle?" After sharing the book encourage your child to find things in the house that are one of the three shapes. He or she can cut pictures from magazines that are circles, triangles and squares and paste them on paper.

I'm Going on a Bear Hunt by Sandra Stroner Sivulich always delights young children. Read through the book several times sharing the excitement of a bear hunt. Then lay the book aside and help your child to use motions to go on the hunt. Swish through the jungle grass. Climb a tree. Then "Oh no! It's a bear! Run!" Help your child to remember the reverse order of events.

Keep in mind that through these kinds of experiences the child's knowledge and mental structure are expanding. Through these and other types of questioning activities found in this book you can become aware of your child's level of reasoning. His or her intellectual growth will emerge as you provide experiences that fit his or her level of understanding.

The book descriptions which follow include some of the best examples of picture books to introduce the young child to the thought processes of conservation, seriation, classification and reversibility. Once you are comfortable with identifying the process you will find many more titles in the picture book section of the public library which touch upon these same processes. Your child's developing ability to understand and use these four types of thinking and his or her success in school go hand-in-hand.

References

Ginsburg, H. and Opper, P. *Piaget's Theory of Intellectual Development.* Prentice-Hall, 1969.

Suggested Children's Reading

Conservation

Balian, Lorna. *The Aminal.* Illus. by the author. Abingdon, 1980. (Ages 4–7).
   Patrick was having a picnic when he saw "The Aminal." He put it in his empty lunch bag. On the way home he met Molly and told her about the Aminal. "It's round and green and blinky-eyed with lots of prickly toenails and a waggy tail," Patrick told her.
   Molly tells Calvin who passes it on to another friend. And so the description of the Aminal is passed on from friend to friend. However, as the news travels, the Aminal grows bigger and bigger and becomes hungrier and hungrier. The friends decide they must protect little Patrick, only to find the Aminal is a turtle.

_____. *Humbug Witch.* Illus. by the author. Abingdon, 1965. (Ages 4–7).
   "Humbug Witch" looked like most witches with a very big nose, two crooked teeth, stringy red hair, a black pointed hat, black shawl, funny-looking black shoes and more. She had a broom and a cat named Fred. However, she was a very little witch, and when she tried to do the magical things all witches can do, they never worked. And so she finally gave up.
   It is surprising to the young reader to find at the end that underneath all the witchy clothes and red hair and a mask, there is a cute little girl who goes to bed.

Cauley, Lorinda Bryan. *The Animal Kids.* Illus. by the author. G.P. Putnam's Sons, 1979. (Pre-sch.–2).
   Four kids think of a way to crash a party where only animals are allowed. In animal costume they eat, play games and have fun thinking they have fooled the animals. When the party is over, the animals take off their animal costume and exclaim, "They didn't even suspect! Yeah, kids aren't so smart!"
   The illustrations in this book are excellent, being large, colorful and expressive. Young children will enjoy this book, especially the surprise ending.

Gantor, Jack. *Swampy Alligator.* Illus. by Nicole Rubel. Windmill, 1980. (Ages 4–7).
   Swampy Alligator lives in a slimy, smelly swamp. Today is his birthday and he hopes his friends will have a party for him. He hasn't seen them in a long time and cannot figure out why. Swampy gets his invitation to his own party from the post-turtle who mentions that it is sure smelly around there, but Swampy thinks everything smells fine.
   As the day progresses there are many animal friends Swampy meets and they all complain about Swampy's appearance and smell in some way. Poor Swampy cannot believe he is smelly or dirty. He is very happy just as he is. He really does not like water or being clean, he seems to think that would not be him if he were clean.
   The friends give Swampy a surprise bath before the birthday party. There are in for a surprise themselves when they find out Swampy is not brown but green. Swampy finds out being clean is not so horrible and also notices his friends stay around him longer and they have a grand time.

Gardner, Beau. *The Turn About, Think About, Look About Book.* Graphics by Beau Gardner. Lothrop, Lee and Shepard, 1980. (Ages 4–6).
   There are graphic shapes on each page. As the page is turned there is a description of what it might be from that angle. The child should soon realize that the same

shape can look like many things but the shape itself has not changed. The child should also have fun making up his or her own description of the shape each time the page is turned.

Hazen, Barbara Shook. *Even If I Did Something Awful.* Illus. by Nancy Kincade. Atheneum, 1981. (Ages 4-7).

A young girl accidentally breaks a vase. Before telling her mother what happened, she asks her mother if she would still love her even if she did something awful. She gives her mother examples of awful things such as pulling down the dining room curtains. Her mother replies that she would love her even if she pulled down the Empire State Building, but she would have to clean it up.

When convinced her mother will love her no matter what, she tells her about the vase. Her mother says that she will be mad and yell at her and then cry a little and pick up the pieces, which the little girl helps her do. But her mother still loves her no matter what.

Hutchins, Pat. *Changes, Changes.* Illus. by the author. Macmillan, 1971. (Ages 3-6).

How many things can you build with blocks? This delightful and colorful book uses no words to stimulate a child's imagination in the many uses of simple building blocks.

_____. *Clocks and More Clocks.* Illus. by the author. Macmillan, 1970. (Ages 4-7).

Mr. Higgins found a clock in his attic, but he didn't know if the time was correct. So he bought another clock, which he placed in his bedroom. The bedroom clock said 3:00. Upon reaching the attic, that clock said 3:01. Now Mr. Higgins didn't know which of these two clocks was correct, so he bought two more clocks. But as he went from clock to clock to check the time, none of them had the same time.

He then brought the Clockmaker to his house, who checked each clock by his watch and found them all to be correct. Mr. Higgins went out and bought a watch, and since then all of his clocks have been correct.

Sasaki, Isao. *Snow.* Illus. by author. Viking, 1982. (Ages 3-6).

Snow is a beautiful picture book. It is made up of a series of pictures in which the same scene is used, but objects, animals and people are added and subtracted from the scene. The time of day also changes from morning to night. The snow continues to fall throughout the day. It is the same yard with the same house, but the other objects are manipulated about.

Ungerer, Tomi. *Crictor.* Illus. by author. Harper and Row, 1958. (Ages 4-7).

Crictor is a good example of a book that illustrates conservation. Crictor is a snake. He can be almost any shape. He can roll up into a ball and make himself into many other shapes. He writes the alphabet with his body and counts by crawling into the shape of the numerals 0 through 8.

The illustrations are well done.

Classification and Seriation

Allen, Pamela. *Bertie and the Bear.* Illus. by author. Coward-McCann, 1986. (Ages 4-7).

Because the bear was chasing Bertie, all the people in the palace, from the Queen to the little dog, got excited. As each new character makes a new noise the din increases until the bear stops, turns around and thanks everyone for the nice welcome!

_____. *Who Sank the Boat.* Illus. by author. Coward-McCann, 1985. (Ages 4–7).
In a small house by a river lived a number of animals. One day they decide to get in the boat (a very small rowboat). As each animal steps in, the boat sinks lower and lower. Finally when the last animal (a mouse) jumps in the boat sinks. Filled with delightful rhythms and bold illustrations!

Anno, Mitsumasa. *Anno's Counting Book.* Illus. by author. Thomas Y. Crowell, 1977. (Ages 3–6).
Without using words the author introduces counting and number systems by showing mathematical relationships in nature. As each numeral (0–12) is introduced, the reader has to search for the objects that match that numeral.
The book begins with a winter scene. There is an empty snow covered field and an empty blue sky representing zero. As the number increases the objects in the picture increase.
The seasons also change as the number grows until the reader is back to winter at the end of the book.

Brown, Ruth. *The Big Sneeze.* Illus. by author. Lothrop, 1985. (Ages 3–6).
Farmer Brown was taking a nap when a fly landed on his nose and he sneezed. This sets off a chain of events that lead to confusion and chaos in the barn. A fun tale, beautifully illustrated.

Carle, Eric. *The Grouchy Ladybug.* Illus. by author. International Copyright Union, Italy, 1977. (Ages 4–7).
A grouchy ladybug refuses to share some aphids with a friendly ladybug. When asked if she wanted to fight for them, the grouchy ladybug replies, "You're not big enough for me to fight."
At 6:00 that morning the grouchy ladybug asks a yellow jacket to fight. Upon seeing its stinger, the ladybug claims the yellow jacket is not big enough to fight.
Each hour through the day she meets a larger animal but always says they're not big enough to fight. At 5:00 she tells the whale he is not big enough, and at 5:45 the whale's tail slaps her, and at 6:00 she lands next to the friendly ladybug again and agrees to share the aphids.
The sequencing of time and the graduation in the size of the animals are good examples of seriation.

_____. *1, 2, 3, to the Zoo.* Illus. by author. Collins-World, 1968. (Ages 3–6).
This delightfully illustrated book takes the reader car by car along a zoo train. The car behind the engine is carrying one elephant. Two hippos ride on the next car with the last car carrying ten birds.
As each page is turned the next brightly illustrated car is seen with a large numeral telling how many animals are aboard. A small zoo train runs across the bottom of the pages increasing as each car is added.
The last page shows all the animals from the train in their proper place in the zoo.

_____. *The Very Hungry Caterpillar.* Illus. by author. Philomel/Putnam, 1981. (Ages 3–7).

The little caterpillar eats through a variety of foods increasing the amounts from Monday to Saturday. After a bad stomachache, he eats a green leaf on Saturday and then begins the processes necessary to become a beautiful butterfly.

Elting, Mary, and Folsom, Michael. *Q Is for Duck.* Illus. by Jack Kent. Houghton Mifflin/Clarion, 1980. (Ages 3–6).

The young reader is challenged as he reads this book to guess the reason why A is for Zoo, B is the Dog, C is for Hen, and D is for Mole. There is a question for every letter of the alphabet.

Every child will be delighted with this book. He or she will learn to classify according to letter, and learn characteristics of animals while saying his ABC's. "Q is for Duck. Why? Because a Duck Quacks."

Fox, Mem. *Hattie and the Fox.* Illus. by Patricia Mullins. Bradbury, 1987. (Ages 2–5).

Big bold pictures tell the tale of Hattie the hen who sees two eyes in the bushes, then two feet, a tail, a body and ears until finally the whole figure, a fox, jumps out. Each animal responds to her warning in the same sequence until the end when each changes its response having seen the fox.

Freschet, Berniece. *Where's Henrietta's Hen?* Illus. by Lorinda Bryan Cauley. G.P. Putnam's Sons, 1980. (Ages 4–7).

One morning Henrietta's hen is not in her box. In each place that Henrietta looks, she encounters a different grouping of animals. At the pond she sees two goats, three ducks and four frogs, but no little red hen. (This provides an excellent opportunity for practice in numerical operations.)

The little hen is finally found sitting on a nest by the haystack. Left alone one day the hen appears in the barnyard followed by one, two, . . . eight baby chicks.

Hoban, Tana. *A, B, See!* Photographs by the author. Greenwillow, 1982. (Ages 3–7).

This informative book for the young reader is not just an A, B, C book as one can *see* in the title. Each page contains a collection of photographs (something to see) that begins with a particular letter of the alphabet. The entire alphabet is repeated on each page showing where the letter for that group of pictures appears in the alphabet. This book is an excellent learning took for any pre-schooler.

_____. *More Than One.* Photographs by the author. Greenwillow, 1981. (Ages 4–7).

Through the use of photographs and ten collective nouns to illustrate each photo, the author shows people, animals and things which are described, for example, as a group, a bunch, a crowd and a flock. The most obvious word that describes the picture is in large blue letters.

_____. *Round and Round and Round.* Photographs by the author. Greenwillow, 1983. (Ages 2–4).

Round and Round and Round will stimulate the children to begin the process of grouping and classifying. Each large colorful picture presents something round for the children to see, such as a ball, peas and a bubble. Another way to stress classification through this book would be to ask how other groups could be formed from the round things?

Hoberman, Mary Ann. *A House Is a House for Me.* Illus. by Betty Fraser. Penguin, 1978. (Ages 4–7).

This book is written in a rhythmic verse that describes all kinds of houses. The illustrations are bright and interesting. The book is fun to read and stretches the imagination. Children will learn what makes a house a house. It is an excellent book for classification purposes as well as stimulating creativity.

Kessler, Ethel, and Kessler, Leonard. *Two, Four, Six, Eight: A Book About Legs.* Illus. by Leonard Kessler. Dodd, Mead, 1980. (Ages 4–7).

A variety of creatures are depicted that have two, four, six or eight legs and even some with no legs. Many two-legged animals, including humans, are named along with the many, many uses of two legs (running, dancing, marching, hopping).

The authors go on to name four-legged, then six-legged, and eight-legged animals along with the uses for these legs.

Mathews, Louise. *Cluck One.* Illus. by Jeni Basett. Dodd, Mead, 1982. (Ages 4–7).

Mrs. Cluck proudly announces that she has laid her first egg. The weasel sighs as Mr. Cluck boasts that the new chicken will crow as loudly as he does. That evening a cuckoo quietly rolls her egg into the Clucks' nest giving the weasel an idea.

Each night the weasel mischievously places another egg in the Clucks' nest, and each morning Mr. Cluck brags about the new egg his wife laid, until Cluck Six had been placed there.

At last the eggs begin to hatch one at a time — first the chick, second the cuckoo, third the duck, fourth the peacock, fifth an ostrich and sixth a turtle. The weasel laughs at the Clucks' silly family and even points out that the little chick won't crow, because it is a hen. To the dismay of the weasel, Mr. Cluck boasts that his children can make a tremendous racket each in his own way.

Not only are the eggs counted in the story as they hatch, but the row of interesting eggs is illustrated at the bottom of the pages, showing each as it hatches with its corresponding ordinal number. These are excellent examples of seriation.

Robart, Rose. *The Cake That Mack Ate.* Illus. by Maryann Kovalski. Little, Brown, 1988. (Ages 2–5).

"This is the cake that Mack ate. Here is the hen that laid the egg that went into the cake that Mack ate." As each ingredient is added, including the farmer that grew the seed and the woman that married the farmer, we finally meet Mack . . . a playful dog, who, to the dismay of the farmer's wife, ate the cake.

Tafuri, Nancy. *The Ball Bounced.* Illus. by author. Greenwillow, 1989. (Ages 3–5).

One day the ball bounced. The cat jumped, the dog barked, the ball rolled. That was the beginning. In sun-drenched pictures and only 33 words, Nancy Tufari tells a story filled with cliffhangers and excitement.

Ward, Cindy. *Cookie's Week.* Illus. by author. Putnam, 1988. (Ages 2–4).

A simple story which shows Cookie the cat getting into trouble on each day of the week and finally resting on Sunday.

Winthrop, Elizabeth. *Shoes.* Illus. by William Joyce. Harper and Row, 1985. (Ages 2–4).

In delightful rhythmic verse, shoes are described by what one does with them: "There are shoes to buckle, shoes to tie, shoes too low and shoes too high, shoes to slide in, shoes for skating." Young children will delight in the combination of verse and bright pictures.

Reversibility

Asch, Frank. *Bear Shadow*. Illus. by author. Prentice Hall, 1985. (Ages 3–5).
Bear's shadow scares a fish away so Bear is determined to get rid of it, yet everywhere he goes his shadow goes and everything he does, his shadow does.
This gentle book will help children to understand that no matter how the shadow changes form it is still the bear's shadow.

Hogrogian, Nonny. *One Fine Day*. Illus. by author. Collier-Macmillan, 1971. (Ages 4–7).
This rhythmic tale of a greedy fox's adventure will delight the young listener. The fox loses his tail because he drank all the milk in the old woman's pail. The old woman cries, "Give me back my milk, and I'll give you back your tail."
The fox asks the cow for milk, who says she will give him milk only if he brings her grass. And so it goes with everything he meets, until he finds the miller who feels sorry for him. He gives the fox the grain to give to the hen to get the egg . . . and on and on until he gives the old woman the milk and she sews his tail in place.
This is an excellent example of reversibility and an ideal story to have the young child try to recall to whom each item goes.

Hutchins, Pat. *Don't Forget the Bacon*. Illus. by author. Greenwillow, 1976. (Ages 3–6).
This is a delightful book. It is humorous and yet realistic.
The story begins with a mother telling her child to go get some things from the

grocery store. As the child walks to the store, he repeats the list over and over in an attempt to remember everything on the list. However, each time he repeats the list, the items change in relation to things he sees on the way. When he arrives at the store, he realizes that he does not know what he is to buy. He retraces his steps in an effort to remember.

————. *1 Hunter*. Illus. by author. Greenwillow, 1982. (Ages 3–6).

One hunter walks through the forest and is seen first by two elephants, then three giraffes, and so on, up to ten parrots. The hunter then turns around and is shocked to see ten parrots, nine snakes, eight monkeys, etc., looking at him.

This book has bright, colorful and interesting illustrations that will delight the young reader.

————. *The Surprise Party*. Illus. by author. Macmillan, 1969. (Ages 4–7).

Rabbit tells Owl that he is having a party tomorrow, and it is a surprise. Owl passes the word to Squirrel that Rabbit is "hoeing the parsley" tomorrow and it is a surprise. As each animal passes the news to another there is a slight change in the interpretation.

The next day as Rabbit asks each animal to come with him, they say, "No, thank you." Last of all, in frustration, Rabbit yells at Owl, "I'M HAVING A PARTY." Now everyone hears clearly, and the party turns out to be a wonderful surprise.

Jonas, Ann. *Round Trip*. Illus. by author. Greenwillow, 1983. (Ages 3–6).

The illustrations are done in black and white. The book is extraordinary in that it is to be read first right side up for the trip to the city and then upside down for the trip back home. The illustrations are to be seen in like manner.

The story records a one day trip to the city and back home.

Peek, Merle. *Roll Over—A Counting Book*. Illus. by author. Houghton Mifflin/Clarion, 1981. (Ages 4–7).

The book begins with, "Ten in the bed and the little one said; Roll over! Roll over! They all rolled over and one fell out." As the story progresses, each time the little one shouts roll over, they all do so causing one more to fall out. This continues until the little one is "alone at last."

The last page contains sheet music and words so that it may be done as a song. The illustrations are nicely done. The words appear in large print.

Quackenbush, Robert. *The Most Welcome Visitor*. Illus. by author. Windmill, 1978. (Ages 4–7).

Fred Horny Toad moves into his new house and he is all alone until one by one his relatives come to visit. Soon there are so many that they practically crowd him out of his own house. Finally, one day, someone appears who causes each of his relatives to leave—one by one—until once again he is all alone.

Sendak, Maurice. *Where the Wild Things Are*. Illus. by author. Harper and Row, 1963. (Ages 4–7).

Mr. Sendak's story is well illustrated and exciting. The main character, Max, starts out acting wild and, when sent to his room, strange things occur which take him on an adventurous journey. At first, Max is thrilled with the changes in his life. Soon, however, he becomes lonely for home and his loved ones. He retraces his steps and ends up back home.

Seuss, Dr. *And to Think That I Saw It on Mulberry Street*. Illus. by author. Vanguard, 1937. (Ages 4–8).

In this enduring classic Marco's hope is to have a grand story to tell his father after school about all of the things he saw that morning; yet, all he sees is a horse and a wagon on Mulberry Street. Marco's determined to have a good story so he begins to add things one by one to make the story a little more interesting. The illustrations tell the story as the pages begin to look more crowded with each added detail. By the time Marco returns home from school, he has created an outlandish tale, yet when his father asks him what he had seen on his way to school, he replies, "A horse and wagon on Mulberry Street."

Wells, Rosemary. *A Lion for Lewis.* Illus. by Atha Tehon. Dial, 1982. (Ages 4–7).

When Lewis played dress-up with his older brother and sister, he was always given the least desirable part, such as, the baby when they were the father and mother or the patient when they were the head nurse and doctor.

Lewis gets in a large lion suit he finds in the attic and scares his brother and sister. This makes Lewis the king.

Yolen, Jane. *An Invitation to the Butterfly Ball.* Illus. by Jane Breskin Zalben. *Parents* magazine, 1976. (Ages 4–8).

The animals from one little mouse to ten little porcupines are invited to the Butterfly Ball.

This delightful book is written in rhyme repeating the rhymes in reverse order as each group of animals (from one to ten) receive invitations.

3

The Path
to Academic Success

The overdevelopment of the functions of the left brain, and the conse-
quent neglect of the right brain may be due in the United States to the
struggle to ensure literacy across the land. Unfortunately, the potential
strengths of the right brain which could serve to improve the basic skills
of reading have not been developed! — Adelhardt and Merrill.

Reading is a whole brain process. The left, verbal side of the brain
decodes the words but the right, visual side of the brain "turns on the movie
show in the head!" Without a mental picture created by words, there is no
meaning. Children drilled in vocabulary lists — words without context —
may learn to recognize individual words but never put them together to
create meaning.

In our knowledge of how the young child's brain develops we know
that all abilities do not develop at the same time and that the last major ability
to develop is that of reading. Parents who attempt to force early reading on
a child whose neurological systems are not ready for the task are setting the
child up for frustration and failure.

Those adults who grew up with radio learned to visualize language as
it was heard. This skill at visualization transferred to the written word as
authors created mental pictures for the reader. Thus, understanding of
print requires a combination of decoding and visualization skills. In addition, the reader's experience plays a vital role in both comprehension and
interpretation of the written word.

Visual Communication

Visual communication can best be defined by a look at the specific
skills involved. Certainly perception and awareness are key components in
its development. This includes perception of graphic forms, color, shadings/

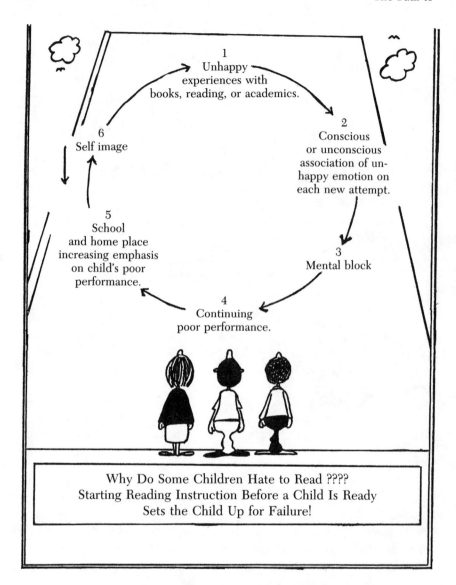

1
Unhappy
experiences with
books, reading, or academics.

2
Conscious
or unconscious
association of un-
happy emotion on
each new attempt.

6
Self image

5
School
and home place
increasing emphasis
on child's poor
performance.

3
Mental block

4
Continuing
poor performance.

Why Do Some Children Hate to Read ????
Starting Reading Instruction Before a Child Is Ready
Sets the Child Up for Failure!

light contrasts, figures, patterns and detail. Numerous books highlight these components.

Tana Hoban's *Take Another Look* (Greenwillow, 1989), is an excellent example of a book which will help young children to perceive and be able to contrast and identify items by size, shape, texture and pattern. In addition, shadings and light form the basis of her more recent book for primary children, *Shadows and Reflections* (Greenwillow, 1990), in which she helps children look not just with their eyes, but with their minds and hearts and imaginations.

The master of detail, Mitsumasa Anno, provides a wealth of visual experiences for children and adults in his *In Shadowland* (Orchard, 1988). With a brief poetic text and richly hued and detailed paintings, Anno brilliantly evokes a spirit rich in dream imagery. Even the most visually literate viewer will need many hours with this and other of Anno's books to savor all that the artist has provided.

Helping younger readers to look more closely is the Ahlbergs' book, *Each Peach Pear Plum* (Viking, 1979). It invites children to play "I Spy" and find the semi-hidden nursery rhyme characters in each of the appealing water-color illustrations.

The visually literate person understands how messages and moods are communicated through art. He or she is able to interpret action in illustration, react verbally to visual work, can read simple body language and can identify work which communicates specific mood. Among books that lead to multiple interpretations are John Goodall's *Red Riding Hood* (1989), *Story of a Castle* (1986) and *Story of a Main Street* (1987), all published by Atheneum.

Raymond Briggs brings both action and mood to the viewer in his wordless story of the poignant relationship of a small boy and a snowman in *The Snowman* (Random, 1979). In describing *The Snowman* as a visual tour, *Horn Book Magazine* says: "Again, as in *Father Christmas* (Coward, 1973), the artist develops narrative, plot and characterization in a sequence of blocks and strips, which at moments of dramatic intensity expand into full-page scenes or double-page spreads. Softly textured pictures in mellow, subdued color add a lyrical quality to the story as it rises and falls to an inevitable end."

As Anno is the master of detail so is Ed Young a master of mood. In *Lon Po Po, the Chinese Red Riding Hood* (Philomel, 1989) the artist evokes a whole series of moods from terror to joy with his evocative illustrations.

The visually literate person can identify simple symbols and their meaning, can verbalize the meanings of symbols used in place of words and can interpret symbolic relationships and creative meaning from symbols. Ed Young's illustrations in *White Wave* (Crowell, 1979) are excellent examples of symbolic representation as well as an artistic achievement of mood. How many readers will note the similarity in shape of White Wave's hair and the temple spires? For those who do see, few will take that next step toward symbolic awareness unless helped to do so.

A masterful achievement of symbolism for older readers is Molly Bang's *Grey Lady and the Strawberry Snatcher*. Here is a perfect blending of the elements of nature and of human nature. Symbolism is evident not only in the figures of the story but in the subtle shadings and light sources.

In one illustration near the end of the book, a tablecloth recounts nearly all of the story events.

Verbal Communication

Talk about the books you and your child share together. Research by Chomsky and by Cazden tells us that reading books aloud and talking about them stimulates children's oral language development. Children take over the language they hear and use it as a part of their own. Listening to and talking about stories is significantly related to the acquisition of literacy.

Look for and share books with rhythmic or repeating patterns. The ability to see patterns and relationships lies in the lower left quadrant of the brain. Pattern books stimulate growth in this quadrant as well as the verbal upper left quadrant and the visual and feeling right quadrants.

In Pat Hutchins's delightful *Don't Forget the Bacon* (Mulberry, 1989), a little boy sets out for the store with a list from his mother. "Six farm eggs, a cake for tea, a pound of pears, and don't forget the bacon."

On his way he repeats, "Six fat legs . . . a cape for me . . . a flight of stairs . . . and don't forget the bacon." Or was it "six clothes pegs . . . a rake for leaves . . . a pile of chairs . . . and don't forget the bacon?" Well, at least he was sure to remember the bacon and so will your preschooler as you laugh together over this delightful book.

Your child will soon chime in on the repeating pattern in Nancy Polette's *The Little Old Woman and the Hungry Cat* (Greenwillow, 1989). With a slip, slop, slurp, the hungry cat ate everything in sight. First the 16 cupcakes in their cups that the little old woman had just baked, then a one-legged man with a squealing pig, followed by a wedding procession, bride, groom, horses and all, and finally the little old woman herself. This is a rib-tickling cumulative tale that the child will soon be able to repeat word for word.

Share counting books with the very youngest. There are many delight-ful titles to choose from. One of the newest and best is *One Crow* by Jim Aylesworth (Lippincott, 1988).

> One crow sits
> on a telephone wire.
> Summer sun's up
> And climbing higher.

And so begins a busy day on a farm. Verse by verse, barnyard animals are introduced in easy-to-count groups — two squirrels chase in a hollow tree, three puppies romp and wag their tails, four kittens roll in the tall milkweeds—until finally as the sky starts to fill with the colors of the setting sun, ten small children play in a grassy field.

Then summer turns to winter, and another busy day on the farm begins. The things to count remain the same—from one crow to ten children—but now the world around them has turned snowy and cold and the things they do have changed with the season. This book introduces many ideas in addition to counting and can be shared and talked about again and again.

Share poetry with all of its cadences and rhythms. Begin with *Mother Goose.* A particularly beautiful new edition is *The Glorious Mother Goose,* selected by Cooper Edens with illustrations by the best artists from the past (Atheneum, 1988). Generation after generation, Mother Goose lives on. Over the years, these rhymes—wise, charming, often nonsensical—have worked their simple music into the hearts and memories of children who themselves have passed on the verses to children of their own. This particular edition is a feat for the eye bringing some of the best illustrations by a wide variety of well-known illustrators. It is a book to be treasured by the child who, with a loving parent, is being introduced to Mother Goose for the first time.

Children in the primary grades enjoy concrete poetry, a poem shaped like its topic or subject. After looking at and hearing *Seeing Things* by Robert Froman (Harper and Row, 1987) young artists will try drawing their own poems.

Share books that help build a strong working vocabulary. The illustration in the parent/child activity on page 32 is adapted from Anne Rockwell's *Albert B. Cub and Zebra.* How many "B" words can you and your child find together? They don't all have to be nouns. Example: It is a "beautiful" day at the "beach." In Anne Rockwell's book there are 26 full color illustrations, one for each letter of the alphabet. What a glorious, language-building search you will have.

Select books to share which are rich in language. Don't be concerned if the child does not understand every word. Fine children's authors use rich language in creating wonderful mental images. The child will understand what is happening. In the Lindenwood College Laboratory school, a group of three-year-olds are introduced to a Rudyard Kipling story for the first time. They nodded their heads to the rhythm of the list of fishes in the ocean . . . the place and the dace, the mackerel and the pickerell and the really, truly twirly, whirly eel." When the mariner in the story was swallowed by the whale and found himself deep down inside the whale's "warm, dark cupboards," the children listened with awe as the mariner solved the problem, being a man of infinite wisdom and sagacity." Three of the Kipling *Just So Stories,* illustrated by Jonathan Langley, were published with a fresh look by Philomel in 1988. These small gems include *How the Rhinoceros Got His Skin, How the Camel Got His Hump* and *How the Whale Got His Throat.*

Bb

How many "B" words can you find in the picture? Look for action words and describing words as well as name words.

This author is the first to admit that there is nothing earthshaking or new about any of these suggestions for assuring academic success for children. What is new is that we now know that these are the kinds of experiences that cause actual neural connections to form in the developing mind of the young child. During the past 15 years a revolution has taken place in what we know about children learning to read. This revolution is seen in the whole language movement which is sweeping the country. To those who embrace the whole language philosophy, learning begins with the experience of the child. The child then creates his or her own meaning in making connections with the written word. Traditionally reading has been considered a process of looking at and putting together parts to achieve the whole. The revolution in reading looks at the process as a whole . . . beginning with the entire story or poem, linking it to the child's prior knowledge and moving to the parts (word attack skills, phonics, etc.) only after the whole is understood.

References

Adelhardt, Denise R. and Merrill, Dale O. *Back to the Basics? Let's Do It Better with the Arts.* Goleta Union School District, 1976.

Cazden, Courtney B. *Child Language and Education.* Holt, 1972.

Cohen, Dorothy H. "Effect of Literature on Vocabulary and Reading Achievement." *Elementary English*, Vol. 45, Feb. 68, 209–213, 217.

Chomsky, Carol. "Stages in Language Development and Reading Exposure." *Harvard Educational Review*, 1972, 1–33.

Healy, Jane. *Your Child's Growing Mind.* Doubleday, 1987.

Thorndike, Robert L. *Reading Comprehension: Education in Fifteen Countries.* Holstead Wiley, 1973.

Wells, Gordon. *The Meaning Makers: Children Learning Language and Using Language to Learn.* Heinemann, 1986.

Suggested Children's Reading

ABC Books

Balian, Lorna. *Humbug Potion: An A.B. Cipher.* Illus. by author. Abingdon, 1984.

Brown, Marcia. *All Butterflies.* Illus. by author. Scribner's, 1974.

Downie, Jill. *Alphabet Puzzle.* Lothrop, Lee and Shepard, 1988.

Elhert, Lois. *Eating the Alphabet: Fruits and Vegetables from A to Z.* Illus. by author. Harcourt Brace Jovanovich, 1989.

Elting, Mary, and Folsom, Michael. *Q Is for Duck: An Alphabet Guessing Game.* Illus. by Jack Kent. Clarion, 1980.

Emberley, Ed. *Ed Emberley's ABC.* Illus. by author. Little, Brown, 1978.

Feelings, Muriel, and Feelings, Tom. *Jambo Means Hello: Swahili Alphabet Book.* Illus. by Tom Feelings. Dial, 1974.

Hague, Kathleen. *Alphabears.* Illus. by Michael Hague. Holt and Co., 1985.

Hoban, Tana. *A, B, See!* Illus. by author. Greenwillow, 1982.

Isadora, Rachel. *City Seen from A to Z.* Illus. by author. Greenwillow, 1983.

Kellogg, Steven. *Aster Aardvark's Alphabet Adventure.* Morrow, 1987.

Lobel, Arnold. *On Market Street.* Illus. by Anita Lobel. Greenwillow, 1981.
MacDonald, Suse. *Alphabatics.* Illus. by author. Bradbury, 1986.
McPhail, David. *Animal A to Z.* Illus. by author. Scholastic, 1988.
Musgrove, Margaret. *Ashanti to Zulu: African Traditions.* Illus. by Leo Dillon and Diane Dillon. Dial, 1976.
Neumeier, Marty and Glaser, Byron. *Action Alphabet.* Illus. by authors. Greenwillow, 1985.
Potter, Beatrix. *Peter Rabbit's ABC.* Warne and Co., 1987.
Provensen, Alice, and Provensen, Martin. *A Peaceable Kingdom: The Shaker Abecedarius.* Viking, 1978.
Rockwell, Anne. *Albert B. Cub and Zebra: An Alphabet Storybook.* Harper and Row, 1977.
Stevenson, James. *Grandpa's Great City Tour: An Alphabet Book.* Illus. by author. Greenwillow, 1983.
Van Allyburg, Chris. *The Z Was Zapped.* Illus. by author. Houghton Mifflin, 1987.

Language Development

Allen, Pamela. *Bertie and the Bear.* Illus. by author. Coward-McCann, 1983 (Ages 2–4).

Because a bear was chasing Bertie, the Queen shouted, "Shoo, shooo, you monster YOU!" and chased the bear. When the king saw what was happening he blew his trumpet, blah! blah! and chased after the Queen. Before long, there were a great many people pursuing the bear, all making an incredible noise — and this had a surprising effect on both the bear and Bertie. A book to appeal to all the senses and to help the child acquire essential language patterns.

Arnosky, Jim. *A Kettle of Hawks.* Illus. by author. Lothrop, 1990. (Ages 4–7).

The terms used to describe wildlife groups tell us something about the animals themselves. Jim Arnosky uses the revealing names of animal groups — a kettle of hawks, a colony of ants, a gaggle of geese — as the starting point for his informative text, illustrated with water-color paintings. As he directs the reader's attention to the sky overhead, the pond, the meadow, the sidewalk beneath our feet, he opens eyes and minds to the wonders of the natural world.

Cole, Joanna. *Miss Mary Mack.* Illus. by Alan Tiegreen. Morrow, 1990. (Ages 3–6).

Here are more than 100 favorite American street rhymes, verses that have been chanted, sung and enjoyed for generations. There are rhymes to make hand clapping and ball bouncing more challenging, plus counting out rhymes to make tag and hide-and-go-seek more exciting. There are also just-for-fun rhymes as well as traditional teases, taunts and comebacks. What a rich language treasury.

Day, Alexandra. *Frank and Ernest.* Illus. by author. Scholastic, 1988. (Ages 6–8).

"Hey, Frank, burn one, take it through the garden, and pin a rose on it." Here is another way of asking for a hamburger with lettuce, tomato and onion! Frank and Ernest, two animal pals learn that in running a diner it's not just what you say but how you say it. Want a hot dog with ketchup and some Jell-o? Well, paint a bow-wow red and get the nervous pudding. How about a tuna on toast and a Dr. Pepper, no ice? How do Frank and Ernest manage to learn all they need to know about running a diner? It's easy as pie! The bear and the elephant not only do a terrific job, but they have a lot of fun. Here is a book full of a secret language children love as well as a story of cooperation and friendship.

_____. *Frank and Ernest Play Ball.* Illus. by author. Scholastic, 1990 (Ages 4–8).
The entrepreneurial duo, Frank and Ernest, take over a baseball team as temporary managers. They must sell tickets, run batting practice, announce the new game and more. And they need to learn baseball lingo fast. Some expressions like "fly hawk" (a skillfull outfielder), "can of corn" (a ball hit so high it's easily caught) no longer sound strange to the animal friends, nor will they to the reader after enjoying this great day in the ballpark.

Demarest, Chris L. *No Peas for Nellie.* Illus. by author. Macmillan, 1988. (Ages 3–6).
Would you rather eat a python than eat your peas? Nellie would. In fact, Nellie would rather eat a furry spider, a hairy warthog, even a slimy salamander! But Nellie's mother and father have laid down the law . . . "No peas, no dessert." A familiar and funny tale for any young child.

de Paola, Tomie. *Tomie de Paola's Book of Poems.* Illus. by author. Putnam's, 1988. (Ages 3–7).
Here are poems ranging from classics by Lewis Carroll, William Blake, Robert Louis Stevenson, Langston Hughes and Robert Frost, to works of modern poets, Jack Prelutsky, Nikki Giovanni, Eve Merriam and Byrd Baylor. There are poems just right for any mood including funny nonsense poems, poems about animals and parents and friends, and quiet bedtime poems to read just before sleep. Language patterns are easy to acquire when found in poetry!

de Regniers, Beatrice, et al. *Sing a Song of Popcorn.* Illus. by author. Scholastic, 1988. (Ages 4–8).
Culled from the work of renowned poets which include Robert Louis Stevenson, Emily Dickinson, Edward Lear and Ogden Nash, these 128 selections are as varied as life itself. There are poems that are funny, some that are touching, some that are profound and some that are pure nonsense. Some are spine-tingling, while others will leave a warm, peaceful glow. Nine different well-known children's artists, including Marcia Brown, Margot Zemach, Maurice, Sendak, Arnold Lobel, Marc Simont, Richard Egielski and the Dillions, have illustrated the poems.

Downie, Jill. *Alphabet Puzzle.* Illus. by author. Lothrop, 1988. (Ages 3–6).
From A to Z, *Alphabet Puzzle* invites young readers to discover the letters of the alphabet and guess the secrets that lie beyond the windows on its pages. "If M is for moon, then N is for ?????" Many guesses can be made before turning the page. A fine associative thinking book to build a rich language storehouse.

Duke, Kate. *Guinea Pigs Far and Near.* Illus. by author. E.P. Dutton, 1984. (Ages 2–4).
Cavorting through the pages, a company of delightful guinea pigs enacts a series of vignettes that will help children discover new word concepts. Here is a book that stretches young imaginations with lots and lots of full-sized illustrations to look at again and again. "Find the guinea pig that is *on* the road." "Which guinea pig is *between* the other two?" The questions can be endless as the child grows in knowledge of place words.

Elting, Mary G. *Q Is for Duck.* Illus. by Jack Kent. Houghton Mifflin, 1980. (Ages 3–5).
Even the youngest child will delight in guessing why A is for Zoo, B is for Dog, and C is for Hen (animals live in a zoo, dogs bark and hens cackle) and this unique approach to learning the alphabet as well as some facts about animals. The questions and answers are easily memorized, so that beginning riddlers can use them — with

or without the book—to play the guessing game with their friends or parents. Whether used as a learning tool or for pure enjoyment at bedtime, *Q Is for Duck* is a book for children who like to have fun while they read or are read to.

Fisher, Aileen. *The House of a Mouse.* Illus. by Joan Sandin. Harper and Row, 1988. (Ages 4–8).

> Do you know, do you know
> where little mice go
> when the meadow is white
> with billows of snow?

Aileen Fisher knows, and in *The House of a Mouse* she answers this and many other questions about the lives, habits and personalities of mice. Throughout this collection of poems the child receives a mouse's-eye view of the world. House-nibbling sheep, ferocious cats, and gigantic humans keep the mice—field mice, house mice, meadow mice, deer mice—alert and the reader amused.

Fraser, Betty. *First Things First.* Illus. by author. Harper and Row, 1990. (Ages 3–5).
      What do you say when you are the first? The early bird catches the worm! What do you say when you are the last? Better late than never!
      This delightful book contains almost two dozen proverbs and explains in words and pictures exactly when to use the right saying. What to say when you have to find out for yourself: Experience is the best teacher. What to say when you don't believe it: Seeing is believing! With colorful pictures filled with detail and humor young children will have a fresh, new look at old familiar sayings.

Gilchrist, Guy. *Night Lights and Pillow Fights.* Illus. by author. Warner, 1990. (Ages 3–5).
      This fun-packed collection of stories, silly rhymes and limericks has something for everyone. There's a monster who is afraid of the dark, a warning of kangaroos who might dare to hop upside down and a salute to the Moodle (a cross between a moose and a poodle). There are also friendly dragons, woolly mammoths and a lovesick old dragon who schemes with Prince Strongheart to win the girls of their dreams. This is a collection sure to delight young readers.

Grossman, Bill. *Donna O'Neeshuck Was Chased by Some Cows.* Illus. by Sue Truesdell. Harper and Row, 1988. (Ages 4–7).

> Donna O'Neeshuck was chased
> by some cows,
> And also by mooses and gooses and sows,
> It happened one day
> When Donna at play
> Patted a cow on the head.

So begins a wild-goose chase as the cow and her friends chase poor Donna all over the place. Why are they chasing her? Donna decides to stop running and find out. A book for lots of laughter!

Guarino, Deborah. *Is Your Mama a Llama?* Illus. by Steven Kellogg. Scholastic Hardcover, 1989. (Ages 3–6).
      Veteran artist Steven Kellogg and author, Deborah Guarino have produced a perfect story hour read-aloud that plays with words.
      "Is your mama a llama?" I asked my friend Dave.
      "No. She is not," is the answer Dave gave.

"She hangs by her feet and she lives in a cave. I do not believe that's how llamas behave."
"Oh," I said. "You are right about that. I think your mama sounds more like a _____."
In riddle rhymes each animal gives hints that help Lloyd and the reader guess who everyone's mama is.

Hayes, Sarah. *Stamp Your Feet: Action Rhymes*. Illus. by Toni Goffe. Lothrop, 1985. (Ages 2–4).
These favorite traditional and modern rhymes are the perfect introduction to responsive play with very young children. Stamp feet on the ground for "The Monster Stomp" or clasp hands and rock to and fro for "Row Your Boat." Step-by-step illustrations demonstrate the actions for each rhyme.

Heller, Ruth. *Kites Sail High*. Illus. by author. Grosset and Dunlap, 1988. (Ages 3–6).
Using simple, lively verse and vivid paintings, this is an imaginative exploration of the world of action words. While clearly aware of the variety of uses and meanings an individual verb may have, the author manages to introduce many basic concepts that are fun to know and think about. A light-hearted rhythmic approach to fun with language!

Hubbell, Patricia. *The Tigers Brought Pink Lemonade*. Illus. by Ju-Hong Chen. Atheneum, 1988. (Ages 4–6).
Is the world a circus parade? From the last day of school through bright summer days to the shivery crispness of an October morning, poems are special. Poems are funny and giggly; poems are thoughts we have and things we do and questions we ask. Should turtles have names? Do mice, in secret, dance madly through the night? Do dragons sass their parents? What makes a sidewalk a special place? Parents and children alike will enjoy this special group of poems that satisfy the child's natural curiosity and tickle the ribs.

James, Betsy. *The Dream Stair*. Illus. by Richard Watson. Harper and Row, 1990. (Ages 4–7).
"When it gets dark, I got to bed and my granny kisses me good night. 'Sweet dreams,' she says. 'Go up the stair, go down the stair, and tell me about it in the morning.'" So begins the adventure of a little girl who climbs the dream stair—first up past chimneys, balloons, and trees to the special attic room with the moon at the window; then down, past furnaces, rivers and roots to the dark safety of the cellar room; and then, finally, back to bed.

Katz, Michael. *Ten Potatoes in a Pot*. Illus. by June Otani. Harper and Row, 1990. (Ages 3–6).
From one cinnamon bun warming in the sun to ten potatoes bubbling in a pot, to a hillside 1500 berries deep, here is a collection of counting rhymes, some familiar and some not. Together the words and the pictures combine to make this a welcome read-aloud rhyming and counting book for young children.

Keller, Holly. *Geraldine's Big Snow*. Illus. by author. Greenwillow, 1988. (Ages 3–5).
"It will come faster if you don't watch so much," said Mama. But Geraldine had a new sled, and she couldn't help watching. And waiting. And hoping the snow would hurry. And when it finally came—in the middle of the night—it was whiter and softer (and better for coasting) than even Geraldine could have imagined. Young children will recognize Geraldine's world as their world and will want to find other titles about this engaging heroine.

Kennedy, X.J. *Fresh Brats.* Illus. by James Watts. McElderry, 1990. (Ages 4–8).
Brent and 41 like-minded brats wreak havoc on others and on themselves in this fresh, irreverent collection of comic verse. Whether they feed growth hormones to a spider or sneak unsavory ingredients into their mother's bread, these young desperados will provide laughs and pleasure to anyone who picks up this book.

Kipling, Rudyard. *How the Whale Got Its Throat.* Philomel, 1989. (Ages 4–8).
Once there was a whale who after eating all the fishes in the sea (except one) swallowed a man of infinite-resource-and-sagacity who had a prowling, howling, hopping, dropping time inside the whale. Not only did the man finally force the whale to take him home but he left him with a surprising reminder of his stay. Every child should be exposed to the rich language of Kipling and here is a delightful means toward that end.

Kovalski, Maryann. *The Wheels on the Bus.* Illus. by author. Little, Brown, 1987. (Ages 2–4).
"The wheels on the bus go round and round, round and round, round and round. The wheels on the bus go round and round, all around the town." Young children will soon be chiming in as they hear this buoyant picture-book adaptation of the well-loved song. The bright illustrations capture all the bustle and funny antics that take place aboard the bus as it tootles around town, making this a bus ride no one will forget.

Livingston, Myra Cohn. *My Head Is Red and Other Riddle Rhymes.* Illus. by Tere LoPrete. Holiday House, 1990. (Ages 2–4).
"Stretch my ribs out wide and high. And I will try to keep you dry." What's being described? An umbrella. Children will have fun guessing the answers to these 27 riddles about dinosaurs, bubble gums, balloons and other objects.

Lloyd, David. *Hello, Goodbye.* Illus. by Louise Voce. Lothrop, 1988. (Ages 2–4).
A big brown bear says, "Hello!" Two bees say, "Hello, hello!" and soon there's a chorus of hello, hello, hello, hello! from the branches of the tree and deep down among its roots. It will be hard for the young child to resist adding his or her own hellos and goodbyes and he/she relates to the antics of the animals in this story. Lots of action, little text, and wonderful pictures to look at again and again.

Lobel, Arnold. *Days with Frog and Toad.* Illus. by author. Harper and Row, 1979. (Ages 3–6).
Frog and Toad enjoy spending their days together. They fly kites, celebrate Toad's birthday and share the shivers when one of them tells a scary story. So when Frog goes off by himself one sunny morning, Toad really worries. He thinks he's lost his friend for good. All turns out well, however, and the child is ready for more adventures with these beloved characters who show what a true friend can be.

McMillan, Bruce. *One Sun: A Book of Terse Verse.* Illus. by author. Holiday House, 1990. (Ages 3–6).
Get ready for a playful day at the beach in this introduction to "terse verse"—a collection of 14 rhymes, each made up of two words that sound alike. After watching a little boy balancing on a "lone stone," finding a "snail trail," and flying a "white kite," you will be inspired to make up your own terse verses.

Maestro, Giulio. *Riddle Roundup: A Wild Bunch to Beef Up Your Word Power.* Illus. by author. Clarion, 1989 (Ages 4–8).
Get ready for more wild and wacky word play. Here are 60 rowdy riddles that will tease minds and tickle funny bones.

What do you call fear of tight chimneys?
When did all the bases get stolen?
To find the answers to these and many more tricky questions, jump right into this roundup of riddles and beef up your word power.

Maris, Ron. *In My Garden.* Illus. by author. Greenwillow, 1987. (Ages 2–4).
Step into the garden. Follow the path to the birdbath and see the frogs in the pool and the field mice in the wall. There's a swing on the tree and a bench near the wall and a big surprise at the end in this gem where the turn of a page lets the child know if his guess was correct.

Morris, Ann. *The Cinderella Rebus Book.* Illus. by Liliana Rylands. Orchard, 1989. (Ages 3–6).
U will C Cinderella win her Prince in this rebus retelling of a favorite fairy tale. Cinderella's fairy godmother, her wicked stepsisters, her pumpkin coach and other familiar characters and objects from the story show up in both the illustrations and the text. Young readers can work out the story to themselves, turning this book into an exciting game that they will come back to again and again.

Prelutsky, Jack. *Beneath a Blue Umbrella.* Illus. by Garth Williams. Greenwillow, 1990. (Ages 4–8).
From the puppies in Philadelphia to the piglets in Wichita, west to the great Salt Lake (where the big green frog lives), and south to the Mardi Gras celebration, here are poems and pictures that provide a verbal and visual tour.

Provensen, Alice and Provensen, Martin. *The Year at Maple Hill Farm.* Illus. by authors. Aladdin, 1978. (Ages 3–6).
A farm year is a cycle of seasons, and seasons are what the animals know. They sense when it is growing cold and begin to prepare for the winter ahead. And when the weather becomes warmer, their pace quickens, because spring makes everything come alive. Here is a year at Maple Hill Farm captured in humorous text and art that both children and adults will treasure.

Rockwell, Anne. *Albert B. Cub and Zebra.* Illus. by author. Harper and Row, 1977. (Ages 3–up).
Someone has abducted Zebra. Albert B. Cub's search for his missing friend takes him all over the world from A to Z. He finds airplanes and apples, babies and balloons, clowns, ducks and Easter eggs. . . . But where, oh where, is poor Zebra? Children and parents will enjoy the search while the child gains facility in beginning sounds and visual discrimination.

Ryder, Joanne. *Lizard in the Sun.* Illus. by Michael Rothman. Morrow, 1990.
Imagine being touched by the sun as it slides into your shadowy room. Imagine growing smaller and smaller, changing your shape until you have four brown feet and a long brown tail. You are a tiny lizard and sometimes you are brown, sometimes green, and sometimes in between as you leap, dash and hide in a world grown immensely large. The author and artist combine to use evocative images to take the reader on a journey into nature. It's remarkable what happens when the world is imagined from another point of view.

Sundgaard, Arnold. *The Lamb and the Butterfly.* Illus. by Eric Carle. Orchard, 1988.
A lamb and a butterfly learn about each other's very different ways of life. "Why do you flutter so?" the lamb asks. "Lambs don't flutter, we walk a straight line. One follows the other."

"But I don't follow anyone," the butterfly replies. "I go wherever I choose." The gentle lamb is both fascinated and alarmed by the daring freedom of the butterfly's life. When a sudden storm soaks and crumples the butterfly's wings, the lamb urges her newfound friend to change his ways and stay with her. "My mother will take care of you," she offers. But will the butterfly settle for security? Here is a subtle message to the very youngest that freedom demands risk-taking but security, too, has its price.

Perceptual Skills

Ahlberg, Allan, and Ahlberg, Janet. *Each Peach, Pear, Plum.* Illus. by authors. Viking, 1979.

Anno, Mitsumasa. *Anno's Alphabet: An Adventure in Imagination.* Illus. by author. Crowell, 1974.

_____. *Anno's Animals.* Illus. by author. Philomel, 1979.

_____. *Anno's Counting House.* Illus. by author. Philomel, 1982.

_____. *Anno's Peekaboo.* Illus. by author. Philomel, 1985.

_____. *Anno's Sundial.* Illus. by author. Putnam and Sons, 1987.

_____. *Topsy Turvies.* Illus. by author. Philomel, 1989.
    Open Anno's witty wordless picture book and find a topsy turvy world where anything is possible. Elflike men swim in a book, suspend from underneath a staircase, hang a picture on the floor and dive off a playing card. Which is up and which is down? What is front and what is back? Where is top and where is bottom? Once again, Anno deftly uses amusing illustrations to stimulate and stretch the minds of readers both young and old to see their worlds anew.

_____. *Upside-Downers.* Illus. by author. Philomel, 1988.
    Welcome to the land of cards, where everyone has an upside-down double. The playful riddling text can be read upside-down or downside-up, or even by two children at once facing each other.

Arnosky, Jim. *In the Forest.* Illus. by author. Lothrop, 1989.
    In the next best thing to an actual walk through a forest with Jim Arnosky at your side, the noted naturalist/artist guides the reader on a tour of the many different environments that make up a forest, pointing out natural phenomena that often go unnoticed. His fascinating and revealing observations are enhanced by a portfolio of stunning oil paintings which he painted during his own visits to the forest.

Aruego, Jose. *Look What I Can Do.* Illus. by author, Scribner's Sons, 1971.

_____, and Dewey, Ariane. *We Hide, You Seek.* Illus. by authors. Greenwillow, 1979.

Base, Graeme. *Animalia.* Illus. by author. Abrams, 1989.
    Animalia is an alphabet book with a difference, a stunning series of images of a fantastic animal world. It is filled with exotic and familiar creatures and everyday things in strange settings, and it is a land with a wealth of hidden objects and ideas.

As you travel from A to Z, each extraordinary scene by Australian artist Graeme Base reveals an ever-expanding world of bizarre detail, and on each new page the details discovered begin with the letter for that page. Thus, H is for Horrible Hairy Hogs, and more. You will also find hamsters and hand-gliders, hippos and hummingbirds, hammocks and horses. And as an added hide-and-seek plus, Graeme Base as a boy is hiding in every illustration. Sometimes he is easy to find, sometimes not. With his bright yellow-and-orange striped sweater you can't miss him — or can you?

Animalia is much more than A is for Apple. The letters of the alphabet explode into images that delight the eye and words that thrill the ear: A is for An Armoured Armadillo Avoiding An Angry Alligator. Here's an incredible imaginary world that will intrigue youngsters of all ages, whether or not they know their ABCs.

Burningham, John. *Come Away from the Water, Shirley.* Illus. by author. Crowell, 1977.

Carle, Eric. *The Secret Birthday Message.* Illus. by author. Harper and Row, 1972.

Carter, David A. *How Many Bugs in a Box?* Illus. by author. Simon and Schuster, 1988.

Crowther, Robert. *The Most Amazing Hide-and-Seek Alphabet Book.* Illus. by author. Viking, 1979.

_____. *The Most Amazing Hide-and-Seek Counting Book.* Illus. by author. Viking, 1981.

Dijs, Carla. *Who Sees You?* at the Zoo. Illus. by author. Grosset and Dunlap, 1987.

Downie, Jill. *Alphabet Puzzle.* Illus. by author. Lothrop, Lee and Shepard, 1988.

Dreamer, Sue. *Animal Walk.* Illus. by author. Little, Brown, 1986.

Drescher, Henrik. *Whose Furry Nose? Australian Animals You'd Like to Meet.* Illus. by author. Lippincott, 1987.

Dubanevich, Arlene. *Pigs in Hiding.* Illus. by author. Four Winds, 1983.

Florian, Douglas. *Nature Walk.* Illus. by author. Greenwillow, 1989.

In a started review of *A Summer Day*, the *ALA Booklist* said, "Florian packs an amazing amount of description into one- and two-word sentences." Come for a nature walk with Douglas Florian as your trail guide and see the truth of these words. Discover the animals, flowers, insects, trees and birds at every bend of the trail — and on every page. There is something to explore wherever you look.

Fox, Mem. *Guess What.* Illus. by Vivienne Goodman. Harcourt, 1990.

Far away from here lives a crazy lady named Daisy O'Grady. She's tall and thin, and she rides a broomstick and wears a pointy black hat, and guess what? She's a witch! Through a series of questions they must answer with a Yes or No, children find out all about Daisy and what she does all day in this captivating picture book. Mem Fox's clear, engaging text, with its rhythmic question-and-answer format and catchy pattern, is perfectly suited for children just learning to read. Vivienne Goodman's uproarious illustrations are packed with wonderfully creepy details that will appeal to every age.

Gardner, Beau. *Have You Ever Seen. . .? An ABC Book.* Graphics by author. Dodd, Mead, 1986.

_____. *The Turn About, Think About, Look About Book.* Graphics by author. Lothrop, Lee and Shephard, 1980.

Goodall, John. *Creepy Castle.* Illus. by author. Atheneum, 1975.

_____. *The Story of an English Village.* Illus. by author. Atheneum, 1979.

Goodall, John S. *The Story of the Seashore.* Illus. by author. McElderry, 1989.
    Since King George III of England took his family to the seaside for their health in the early 1800s, holidays at the shore have been a cherished pastime. Goodall's work captures the seaside holiday in all of its various manifestations from the 19th century to the present. A Punch and Judy show for Victorian children and an afternoon tea at a splendid hotel are depicted with the same loving care as a fun fair at Blackgood and a sailing regatta. Here, told in pictures, is a social history of people's long-standing devotion to sun, sea and sand.

Gould, Deborah. *Terry's Creature.* Illus. by Anatoly Ivanov. Lothrop, 1989.
    A tiny hippopotamus with delicate wings is left over from Terry's dream but he is the only one who knows it for what it is. Then he paints its picture, enabling everyone to share his dream and opens the way to his future as an artist. The text of this story is on one level — the story of a boy's discovery of his own communicative talent. On another level, this book is a powerful metaphor for all artistic creativity.

Heller, Nicholas. *The Front Hall Carpet.* Illus. by author. Greenwillow, 1990.
    A river in the front hall? A grassy field in the dining room? Acres of blinding snow (complete with polar bear and penguins) in the living room? Yes, and much, much more to celebrate the role of fantasy in everyday life. A book to stimulate the imagination and to help children see things in different ways.

Hill, Eric. *Spot Goes to the Circus.* Illus. by author. Putnam, 1986.

Hoban, Tana. *A, B, See!* Illus. by author. Greenwillow, 1982.

_____. *Exactly the Opposite.* Illus. by author. Greenwillow, 1990.
    Brilliant photographs present a world of possible opposites, both open-ended and thought provoking. Are the hands open and closed or are they left and right? Is the hammock empty and full or near and far? You must look and think and decide for yourself.

_____. *Take Another Look.* Illus. by author. Greenwillow, 1981.

Hutchins, Pat. *Which Witch Is Which?* Illus. by author. Greenwillow, 1989.
    Here is the story of Ella and Emma, twins, who go to a costume party dressed as witches. But which witch is which? Hutchins's fans will have no problem figuring this out because there are just enough clues — for the careful observer.

Jonas, Ann. *Color Dance.* Illus. by author. Greenwillow, 1989.
    What happens when you mix red and yellow? How about yellow and yellow? Blue and red? What about blue and blue? Come to the color dance and watch the dancers. They have the answers and so will the reader.

_____. *Reflections.* Illus. by author. Greenwillow, 1987.

_____. *Round Trip.* Illus. by author. Greenwillow, 1983.

_____. *Where Can It Be.* Illus. by author. Greenwillow, 1986.

Kasza, Keiko. *The Pigs' Picnic.* Illus. by author. Putnam, 1989.

Mr. Pig wants to look his best and sets out to ask Miss Pig to go on a picnic with him. He gets all kinds of advice from his friends, the Fox, the Lion and the Zebra, but when he does what they suggest, the effect on Miss Pig is not at all what he intended. How can he persuade her that a picnic with him would be a perfect way to spend an afternoon? What does he look like when he adds to his appearance the distinguishing features of the other animals?

King, Deborah. *Cloudy.* Illus. by author. Philomel, 1990.

A visual hide-and-seek game follows an elusive cat's travels from morning until night. There, nestled in the shadows of a meadow, prowling in the long grass bathed in moonlight, curled up in a deserted stable, Cloudy lives a secret life in these and other enchanting places.

Lobel, Arnold. *The Turnaround Wind.* Illus. by author. Harper and Row, 1988.

Most, Bernard. *Turnover.* Illus. by author. Prentice-Hall, 1980.

Noll, Sally. *Watch Where You Go.* Illus. by author. Greenwillow, 1989.

Things are often not what they seem to be, especially if you are a small mouse. A field of golden grass turns out to be a lion's mane. A tree trunk is really an elephant's trunks. Despite the warnings of a clever dragonfly, the mouse goes his own way to a safe and happy ending.

Raskin, Ellen. *Nothing Ever Happens on My Block.* Illus. by author. Atheneum, 1966.

Roth, Harold. *Let's Look Around the House.* Illus. by author. Putnam, 1988.

_____. *Let's Look Around the Town.* Illus. by author. Putnam, 1988.

Shaw, Charles Green. *It Looked Like Spilt Milk.* Harper and Row, 1947.

Tafuri, Nancy. *Spots, Feathers and Curly Tails.* Illus. by author. Greenwillow, 1988.

Turner, Ann. *Heron Street.* Illus. by Lisa Desimini. Harper and Row, 1989.

Here is a pictorial history of one small part of the United States — a lonely marsh inhabited by herons. The marsh is settled by people and everything begins to change. From the arrival of the Pilgrims to today we see the changes take place; a contrast of progress and the loss of the natural world.

4

The Power of
Fairy Tales and Fantasy

No literature is more suited to the stimulation of every part of the child's brain than fairy tales and fantasy. It is significant that so many outstanding thinkers of our day tell of a childhood rich with fairy tales and fantasy. When Albert Einstein was asked what children should be exposed to that would best help them to become scientists, his response was "fairy tales."

Those of us who have walked through the forest with Red Riding Hood, felt the injustice of Rumpelstiltskin's claim, understood the love that Beauty felt for the beast and experienced the joy of Cinderella when the glass slipper fit, those of us who share this literary background lead richer, fuller lives because of it. It is true that many of the decisions we make as adults are consciously or unconsciously based on the stories we heard as children. Fairy tales are always solidly based on human values. It is rarely the magic sword or enchanted cloak that wins the day, but the inner resources of the human condition that conquer evil and adversity.

Imagination can illumine the real world and make sense out of reality. The world we know ordinarily is limited because it is finite and we are mortal. But we have no need to rein in our imaginations. Contemplate the infinity of ideas available and not yet captured between the pages of a book. Again, Einstein has written, "The fairest thing we can experience is the mysterious. It is the fundamental emotion which stands at the cradle of true art and true science. He who knows it not, who can no longer wonder, can no longer feel amazement, is as good as dead, a snuffed out candle."

In our highly technical world, children are introduced to computers in infancy. They are taken to fire houses, supermarkets, shopping malls, factories and offices. Is equal attention being paid to helping the child grasp the unseen, the intangible? Kornei Chukovsky, the great Russian writer of children's books, has said about early childhood: "The young child uses fantasy as a means of learning, and adjusts it to reality in the exact amounts his

44

need demands. The present belongs to the sober, the cautious, the routine-prone, but the future belongs to those who do not rein in their imaginations."

Fairy tales and fantasy do, indeed, provide stimulation of the whole brain. An excellent example is the beautifully illustrated new edition of Hans Christian Andersen's *The Tinder Box* illustrated by Warwick Hutton and published by Margaret K. McElderry Books in 1988.

For generations, this story by a master teller of tales has been a favorite with children. It tells of a soldier, returning from the wars who—through a chance meeting with an old witch—acquires a tinder box. When he strikes it once, a dog with eyes as big as saucers appears to do his bidding. When he strikes it twice, a dog with eyes as big as mill wheels is instantly there at his command. When he strikes it three times, a huge dog with eyes as big as the Round Tower arrives, ready to do what the soldier asks.

Now it has been foretold that the princess of the kingdom will marry a common soldier. To prevent this, the king keeps her in a walled castle so no one may see her. Though the soldier, with the money he now can acquire through the dogs, has fine clothes, the best lodgings and many friends (because he is generous to all), his greatest wish is to see the princess. The dogs fulfill his wish, but he is discovered and condemned to be hanged. He is saved at the final moment by using his tinder box. As a happy and satisfying ending, the princess is released from the castle, marries the soldier and "the wedding feast lasted for eight days with the three dogs as the guests of honor."

As a master teller of tales, Andersen's rich use of language stimulates the left brain language center. The logical, sequential ordering of events stimulates the lower left quadrant of the brain as do the problems that occur throughout the story and their resolution. The touch of fear when the soldier first meets the witch, the apprehension as he approaches the gallows, and the joy of his rescue all touch the lower right, affective quadrant. The beautiful illustrations, and the creation of the fantasy dogs like no dogs ever before seen are those creative elements that stimulate reaction in the upper right quadrant. While this is only one example of the effect of fairy tales and fantasy on thought, almost every other well-written tale in this genre can do the same.

Creative Thinking

Gerald McDermott adapted *Arrow to the Sun* from a Pueblo Indian tale and powerfully illustrated the story with direct, bold colors of gold, yellow, orange, brown, magenta, green and turquoise against a black background. These strong illustrations tell the story of a boy who came into the world

through a spark of life sent to a young maiden from the Lord of the Sun. Shunned by the other boys because he had no father, Boy went on a journey to seek his father. Corn Planter and Pot Maker could not help him, but Arrowmaker turned the boy into an arrow and shot him to the Sun. Before the Sun would acknowledge him, the boy had to overcome four trials. Surviving the trials, the Lord of the Sun acknowledged his son who returned to earth to dance the dance of life.

SHARING RELATIONSHIPS:
Is this a picture of the sun? How do you know? Could there be other ways to draw the sun? Would you show me? Could a person really travel to the sun? Why or why not? The sun is important in many Indian stories. I wonder why? Do you know? Watch for the patterns you see in the sun on other pages. Can you find the same patterns?

There is no question that exposure to fairy tales and fantasy can stimulate the creative brain. In his definition of creativity, Ned Herrmann states that "Creativity must in the final analysis be whole brained. The elements of the process . . . require all four quadrants of the brain. If any

one of the quadrants is unavailable, then the process tends to fall apart. . . .
If, for example, someone denies their feelings then that kind of feedback
is unavailable to let them know they are on the right track. The individual
who refuses to engage in logical thought or analysis loses the value of that
needed activity when an idea needs to be thought through. The individual
who has never been able to visualize or who feels that fantasy is childish
denies him or herself the kind of mental usefulness that Einstein rates at
the top of his list of mental priorities."

Every fairy tale is a problem solving experience. In Tony Ross's humorous version of *The Boy Who Cried Wolf,* Willy cries "Wolf, wolf!" when he
doesn't want to do something like take a bath or have his violin lesson. Soon
no one pays any attention to him. To the young child this may seem an ideal
way to solve the problem of getting out of something you don't want to do.
However, as in the original fable, Willie's plan backfires. He meets a real
wolf and is in real danger. He runs home to find his grandmother in the yard
hanging clothes. "Wolf, wolf!" Willie cries. "Tell me another one," Grandmother replies. How can Willie be saved now? The only items available are
the clothesline, clothespins, a clothes basket and a sheet.

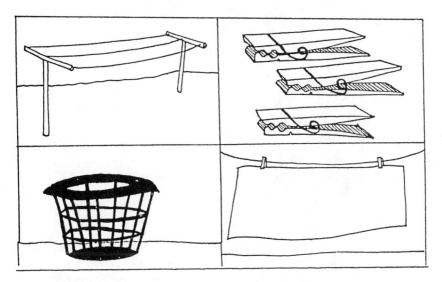

Even the very youngest can explore problem-solving situations in fairy
tales. Faced with the challenge of adding something to the pig's house so
that the wolf could not blow it down, one five-year-old drew a fan in the
door. When asked what the fan would do, the youngster replied that "When
the wolf blows, it will blow his blow right back!"

Fairy tales can create a startling new environment for the mind. Once
a child has ventured beyond earthly restrictions, he or she can never crawl

THREE FAMOUS HOUSES

Only one of the Three Pigs was a good builder. The wolf could not blow down the third house made of bricks!

Here is the first little pig's straw house.

Add things to this house so that the wolf cannot blow it down.

back into old mental modes of thought. While the setting of the tale may be in a fantasy world, the tales themselves are very real indeed. The fairy tale describes the basic human condition and shows how through the effort of the hero or heroine (rather than the magic sword or invisible cloak) adversity can be overcome and truth can triumph. What child, like Cinderella, has not at times felt alone or unloved? What child, like Goldilocks, has not explored forbidden areas and received the consequences? What child, like Red Riding Hood, has failed to heed advice from an adult and ended up in trouble? Some critics say that a child of today cannot comprehend a dragon. That is not true. Many children can and do. But shouldn't all children be given the opportunity to develop the elasticity of the mind to make the attempt? What better skill sharpener than exposure to meaningful tales, for all great books, especially fairy tales and fantasies, teach us about life.

Choices of these mind-stretchers to share with children in the fairy tale realm are almost endless. The Grimm Brothers, Hans Christian Andersen, Charles Perrault, Peter Asbjornsen, Joseph Jacobs, Kenneth Grahame, L. Frank Baum, Lewis Carroll and A.A. Milne are all writers or collectors of these classics of children's literature. The books which follow and which are described in some detail are very recent additions to this literature and examples of the work of contemporary authors or illustrators. They serve as a taste from the rich literary meal available in your public library.

References

Herrmann, Ned. *The Creative Brain.* Applied Creative Services, 1988.
Polette, Nancy, and Hamlin, Marjorie. *E Is for Everybody.* (1st edition). Scarecrow, 1976.
Ross, Tony. *The Boy Who Cried Wolf.* Dial, 1987.

Suggested Children's Reading

Fairy Tales and Fantasy

Andersen, Hans Christian. *Ardizzone's Hans Andersen: Fourteen Classic Tales.* Illus. by Warwick Hutton. McElderry, 1979. (Ages 4–9).

The 14 tales of this selection from the work of Hans Christian Andersen include favorites like *The Snow Queen, The Ugly Duckling, The Tinder Box, The Emperor's New Clothes* and, of course, *The Little Mermaid,* together with one or two of the shorter, less well-known stories, such as *The Shirt Collar.* The book offers a fine sample of the work of Hans Andersen the storyteller and clearly reflects his own approach to life. He never lost his love for the poor people of Denmark, to whom he belonged, and whose rough humor, courage and simplicity he so much admired. Success did not spoil him; he knew that life is never easy and that virtue is not its own reward; that there is a price to be paid for happiness, often too high a one to bear. Andersen's own philosophy of life is the essence of his storytelling.

Asbjornsen, Peter C. *East o' the Sun and West o' the Moon.* Illus. by Gillian Barlow. Philomel, 1988. (Ages 6–8).

In this beloved Norse tale, a great white bear offers a poor peasant family endless wealth in trade for its youngest and most beautiful daughter.

When the girl generously agrees to the mysterious offer, she is quickly taken by the bear to a magnificent mountain castle where she discovers that the bear is an enchanted prince. Too late, she also discovers her love for him, for now she must travel across the world to break the enchantment that keeps him imprisoned East o' the Sun and West o' the Moon.

Brown, Marcia. *Dick Whittington and His Cat*. Illus. by author. Scribner's, 1950. (Reissued, 1988). (Ages 4–7).

"Turn again, Whittington, Lord Mayor of London!!" For many years children all over the world have loved the story of Dick Whittington and his cat—and of the promise rung out by Bow Bells.

This famous old English story of the poor boy who became rich because of his cat, and because he listened to Bow Bells, has endured as long as has Robin Hood.... A winning story for a child.

Marcia Brown, distinguished three-time Caldecott medalist, has retold the famous tale from original sources.

Browning, Robert. *The Pied Piper of Hamelin*. Illus. by Donna Diamond. Holiday House, 1981. (Ages 5–9).

A long time ago, the people of Hamelin had a terrible problem. Rats were everywhere. They dashed through the streets, danced in the doorways and ran through the houses. Everyone was miserable.

The townspeople tried to destroy the rats, but nothing worked. Not even the Mayor could figure out what to do. One day, a stranger with a magic flute offered to rid the town of rats in exchange for money. Unfortunately, the Mayor's greed caused the "Pied Piper" to give the town a much bigger problem than rats. He took away the town's children, never to return.

Clark, Ann Nolan. *In the Land of the Small Dragon*. Illus. by Tony Chen. Viking, 1979. (Ages 6–8).

In the Land of Small Dragon there lived a man and two daughters—Tam and Cam. Tam, the beautiful, good child, was made to work hard by her jealous stepmother, who favored her own child, Cam. But Tam gets help from a fairy godmother, a fish with magical powers and the willing forces of nature. As a reward for her kindness she even acquires a beautiful dress and two jeweled hai (slippers).

One day a small bird drops one beautiful hai in front of the Emperor's son, who is walking in the garden. The Prince decides he must marry the girl whose foot will fit the lovely slipper.

In this charming Vietnamese folktale, retold in the traditional metric form and with proverbs interspersed among the verses, Ann Nolan Clark re-creates an authentic Cinderella variation that will surprise and delight many readers. The dazzling illustrations by Tony Chen are a graceful and appropriate complement to the text.

Clément, Claude. *The Painter and the Wild Swans*. Illus. by Frédéric Clément. Dial, 1986. (Ages 4–8).

Rarely can a book be called unforgettable, but *The Painter and the Wild Swans* is that kind of book.

It is the story of Teiji, a renowned Japanese painter. So fine are his paintings that people travel from all corners of the world to sit for their portraits. Then one winter's day he sees a flock of wild swans pass overhead; in that instant he knows that until he captured the beauty of the birds on canvas, he will not paint again.

His search takes him to a deserted hut, a treacherous ice-filled lake, and a wise old fisherman. Through amazing strength and courage Taiji comes closer and closer to the alluring birds. Finally, magically, they meet. The book has an astonishing outcome which will enthrall readers.

With his exquisite paintings Fréderic Clément has perfectly rendered the Japanese setting of Claude Clément's story. The lavish use of Japanese calligraphy, telling one swan's story, elegantly enhances every page.

Demi. *Demi's Reflective Fables.* Illus. by author. Grosset, and Dunlap, 1988. (Ages 4–8).

A big chow chow hid behind a tree, about to attack a little Pekinese, when the Pekinese trotted right up and stopped him. "Why do you always do this?" he asked. "Because you are so sneaky," the big chow chow replied. "And you are smaller than I am."

"It seems to me," began the Pekinese, "that your brain is like your vision. Your eyes can see things far away, but they cannot see their own lashes. I can't help being small, and I have to be sneaky to fight off such a big dog as you. Reflect on this — you have attacked me many times before, and I have always beaten you. Perhaps you are sneakier, and meaner, too, because you are so much bigger."

The big chow chow hung his head in shame and walked away, vowing never to bother the little Pekinese again.

In this unusual picture book, Demi retells and illustrates 13 ancient Chinese fables so young readers can reflect on them, both figuratively and literally. She includes a mirror on the front jacket flap. After reading each of the charming tales, children can use the mirror to reflect the exquisite pictures.

de Paola, Tomie. *The Legend of the Indian Paintbrush.* Illus. by author. G.P. Putnam's, 1988. (Ages 4–7).

In spring, the hills and meadows of Texas and Wyoming are ablaze with the reds, oranges and yellows of the Indian Paintbrush. How this striking plant received its name is told in an old Indian legend.

Many years ago, when the People traveled the Plains, a young Indian boy had a Dream-Vision in which it was revealed that one day he would create a painting that was as pure as the colors of the evening sky at sunset. The boy grew up to become the painter of the tribe, but although he found a pure white buckskin for a canvas and made paints from the brightest flowers and the reddest berries, he could not capture the sunset.

How the young Indian artist finally fulfills his Dream-Vision is lovingly told and illustrated by Tomie dePaola, in words and pictures that capture the spirit and beauty of this dramatic legend.

Grimm, Wilhelm. *Dear Mili.* Illus. by Maurice Sendak. Farrar, Straus and Giroux, 1988. (Ages 6–9).

On September 28, 1983, the discovery of a previously unknown tale by Wilhelm Grimm was reported on the front page of the *New York Times*. "After more than 150 years, " the *Times* noted, "Hansel and Gretel, Snow-White, Rumpelstiltskin, and Cinderella will be joined by another Grimm fairy-tale character." News of this dramatic find made headlines around the world.

The tale of *Dear Mili* was preserved in a letter Wilhelm Grimm wrote to a little girl in 1816, a letter that remained in her family's possession for over a century and a half. It tells of a mother who sends her daughter into the forest to save her from a terrible war. The child comes up on the hut of an old man, who gives her shelter, and she repays his kindness by serving him faithfully for what she thinks are three days. Actually 30 years pass. When she finally leaves to return to her mother, the old man hands her a rosebud and says, "Never fear. When the rose blooms you will be with me again."

Kamen, Gloria. *The Ringdoves.* Illus. by author. Atheneum, 1988. (Ages 5–9).

One day a wise and mighty crow saw a hunter spread his net and catch a flock of ringdoves. But the king of the doves called out, "Let us unite and fly away together," and the birds flapped their wings in unison and rose with the net. They flew to the burrow of Zirak, the mouse, who gnawed at the net until the doves were free.

Impressed by the friendships of Zirak and the doves, the crow asked the mouse if he, too, could be his friend. The mouse, unwilling at first to trust someone he considered his natural enemy, decided to take the risk.

The story of how the mouse and crow later outwit the hunter in order to rescue their other friends—a tortoise and a gazelle—is one of the classic fables of India. First told in 300 B.C., the Fables of Bidpai have spread from India to all of the Near East, and are known and enjoyed by children in that part of the world.

Gloria Kamen has interpreted one of the tales in pictures glowing with color, to delight and instruct young readers of today.

McAllister, Angela. *The King Who Sneezed.* Illus. by Simon Henwood. Morrow Junior Books, 1988. (Ages 4–7).

High up in the Drafty Mountains, stingy King Parsimonious is too cheap to buy firewood for his crumbling old castle. It's no wonder that his daily dinner of green alphabetti spaghetti always arrives as cold as the cheese and onion milkshake he drinks with it. But one day a draft blows in that even the Royal Hot Water Bottle can't keep out. All the King's Men have the Official Afternoon Off, so Parsimonious himself goes stumbling about in search of the draft that has him sneezing icicles all over the Royal Nose.

There are more chills—and spills—than the King is counting on in Angela McAllister's wacky fable, illustrated with merry majesty by Simon Henwood.

Marshall, James. *Goldilocks and the Three Bears.* Retold and illus. by the author. Dial Books for Young Readers, 1988. (Ages 3–6).

Papa Bear, Mama Bear and little Baby Bear were mighty hungry after their morning ride. But when they returned to their beautiful Victorian home, it was in a terrible state. Their porridge, left cooling on the dining room table, had been eaten. Baby Bear's chair was broken into little pieces. And upstairs the intruder still slept. Who would have thought that one little girl could cause such pandemonium?

James Marshall, original and irreverent as always, enriches this familiar tale with inventive touches that will have readers—both young and old—clutching their sides with merriment.

————. *Red Riding Hood.* Retold and illus. by the author. Dial Books for Young Readers, 1987. (Ages 3–6).

Mother always told Red Riding Hood not to talk to strangers. But the wolf she met on the way to Granny's was so charming and urbane. What could be harm of telling him that she was on her way to Granny's pretty yellow house on the other side of the woods? Who could be a better escort than the big-eyed, long-armed, big-toothed wolf?

The inimitable James Marshall, whom *Publishers Weekly* described as a "specialist in absurdity," embellishes a familiar tale with irreverent flourishes that will have young readers—and their elders as well—rolling with laughter all the way through to the madcap finale.

Mayer, Marianna. *Iduna and the Magic Apples.* Illus. by Laszlo Gal. Macmillan, 1988. (Ages 6–9).

Out of the northern mists comes this timeless tale of the goddess Iduan, whose gift of everlasting life keeps the world young. The divine love that flows from the beautiful Iduna constantly renews the earth, and the golden apples from her sacred garden give immortality to the gods.

But when the previous fruit is stolen and the goddess abducted by an evil giant, a frozen darkness descends upon the world. A journey to the land of the dead and a battle of fire and ice must be undertaken before the wicked are conquered and Iduna can once again reign in her sacred grove.

This ancient Norse myth comes to life again in the haunting words of Marianna Mayer and the exquisitely detailed illustrations of Laszlo Gal.

Polacco, Patricia. *Rechenka's Eggs*. Illus. by author. Philomel, 1988. (Ages 4–7).

Old Babushka, known throughout all of Moskva for her beautifully painted eggs, is preparing her eggs for the Easter Festival when she takes in an injured goose. She names the goose Rechenka, and they live happily together until one day when Rechenka accidentally overturns a basket, breaking all of Babushka's lovingly crafted eggs.

But the next morning Babushka has a surprise awaiting her in the basket. She cries: "A miracle!" It is one of many in this charmingly told tale of friendship and caring.

With vibrant, full-color illustrations, Patricia Polacco has joyously re-created the flavor of Old Moscow and its festivals. The eggs, stunningly colored and intricately designed are authentic reproductions of eggs painted in the Ukrainian style. *Rechenka's Eggs* is a timeless story of classic beauty.

Rockwell, Anne. *Puss in Boots and Other Stories*. Illus. by author. Macmillan, 1988. (Ages 4–7).

"There was once a poor widow who had a son named Jack. . . ." With these words Anne Rockwell draws children and adults into the world of the storyteller, a world of wonder, wisdom and joy that is older than written language yet always fresh and new. In this book she retells in clear, rhythmic language 12 of the most loved stories from "The Miller and His Son" and "Nail Soup" to "Jack and the Beanstalk," "Briar Rose," and "Kate Crackernuts." This is a perfect family book to be shared by parent and child alike.

————. *The Three Sillies*. Illus. by author. Harper and Row, 1979. (Ages 3–6).

Eleven classic nursery tales beloved by children for generations, including such favorites as "The Bremen Town Musicians," "The Tortoise and the Hare," "The Lad Who Went to the North Wind," and "The Old Woman and Her Pig." Rockwell uses lively and rhythmic pose suitable for beginners to read on their own but also fun for parents in read-aloud sessions.

Seeger, Pete. *Abiyoyo*. Illus. by Michael Hays. Macmillan, 1986. (Ages 3–7).

Once there was a little boy who played the ukelele. Wherever he'd go he'd play, Clink, Clunk, Clonk. His father was a magician. Wherever he'd go, he'd make things disappear, Zoop! Zoop! Soon the townspeople grew tired of the boy's noise and his father's tricks, and banished both of them to the edge of town.

There they lived, until one day when the terrible giant Abiyoyo appeared. He was as tall as a tree, and it was said that he could eat people. Everyone was terrified except the boy and his father, and they came up with a plan to save the town. A song that becomes a lively story.

Steele, Flora Annie. *Tattercoats*. Illus. by Diane Goode. Bradbury, 1978. (Ages 4–8).

The girl called Tattercoats ran unhappily from the kitchen to find her friend, the goatherd. He was her only companion, an odd, magical chap who, when Tattercoats was hungry or cold or tired, would play to her so gaily on his little pipe, that she would forget all her troubles and fall to dancing with his flock of noisy geese for partners.

Perhaps he would play to her now. More than anything, she wished she could see the grand doings at the King's ball, where this very night the Prince was to select his bride. But she had merely tatters from the ragbag to wear, and had been left out by her bitter old grandfather who had already set off for the festivities.

The goatheard knew just what to do. "Take fortune when it comes, little one," he said, reaching for her hand and starting her along the way to the King's ballroom. There before the King and the Prince and all the lords and ladies, the goatherd played once again a magical tune—a few notes only, but enough, so that everyone saw Tattercoats for herself.

Van Rynbach, Iris. *The Soup Stone.* Illus. by author. Greenwillow, 1988. (Ages 4–7).

A soldier on the way home from the war stops at a farmhouse to ask for food and shelter. The farmer is poor and says he hardly has enough for his own family. But the soldier announces that he had a soup stone and all he needs is a large pot filled with water. Once the pot is on the stove, with the aid of his wits and the seemingly magic stone, the soldier is able, bit by bit, to coax from the farmer the ingredients for a tasty soup. A fresh and charming rendering of an old story set in post–Revolutionary New England where it seems perfectly at home.

Van Woerkom, Dorothy. *Alexandra the Rock Eater.* Illus. by Rosekrans Hoffman. Knopf, 1978. (Ages 4–8).

In tales where wishes come true, wishes can also get out of hand. When Alexandra and Igor fervently wish for one child to call their own, they are rewarded with not one but one hundred. There is love enough for all of them, just room enough in the small house, but not food enough for so many hungry children and not a penny to buy more.

So, armed with only two small cheeses and a pocketknife, Alexandra heads toward the dark side of the forest, determined to outwit a destructive dragon and capture his gold. In a funny and unusual twist, the dragon turns out to be young and dim-witted, and he decides to take Alexandra home to meet his Momma. Eager to be rid of this pesky woman, Momma sets up three tasks requiring dragon-like strength. But Alexandra proves that bold spirit and good sense can be the greatest power of all. She not only survives but returns triumphant to her family.

Wilde, Oscar. *The Star Child.* Illus. by Fiona French. Four Winds, 1979. (Ages 4–8).

Two woodcutters were making their way home one snowy winter evening when a bright and beautiful star fell out of the sky and into the pine forest before them. They ran toward it, and found not a star, but a sleeping baby wrapped in a cloak of golden tissue. One of the men took the baby home.

The child was brought up with the village children, and every year he grew more beautiful. But he also became vain and selfish. And, as the child of a star, he was filled with overwhelming pride.

One day he accidentally meets his real mother, but when she calls him her son he spurns her because she is old and ugly and clothed in rags. For this cruel act he is transformed into a creature as ugly as a toad. A moving story with beautiful illustrations.

Wood, Don, and Wood, Audrey. *Heckedy Peg*. Illus. by Don Wood. Harcourt, Brace Jovanovich, 1987. (Ages 4–8).

Seven children named Monday, Tuesday, Wednesday, Thursday, Friday, Saturday and Sunday; a witch who intrudes on the peace of their cottage; and a spell only the children's mother can break — these dramatic elements form a story that is both contemporary and timeless. Using full color oil paintings, scenes of home and hearth and the memorable witch's hut come magically to life. Rich in images and delightful details, this story is perfect for bedtime, storytime, anytime.

Yolen, Jane. *The Girl Who Loved the Wind*. Illus. by Ed Young. Thomas Y. Crowell, 1972. (Ages 5–9).

Lovely Danina has never seen anything sad. She is surrounded by happy music, beautiful paintings and always smiling servants. Her wealthy father has so ordered, to keep the daughter he loves from ever being hurt. But even the high walls of the house cannot keep Danina from hearing the voice of the wind. Its song is sometimes sad and harsh, sometimes sweet — like life itself. "Life is not always happy," sings the wind. And once Danina has heard the song, what had once seemed like a palace now feels like a prison. What lies beyond the walls?

5

Developing the
Creative Mind

Creative thinking is a whole brain process. Whether it results in new methods, new procedures or new products, every area of the brain must be used. The upper right quadrant visualizes, creates and intuits, the lower right quadrant inspires and motivates, the lower left quadrant organizes and the upper left quadrant critiques . . . all essential elements in the creative process. Eleanor Duckworth states in her book, *Piaget Rediscovered*, that "The goal of education is to create men who are capable of doing new things, not simply repeating what other generations have done . . . men who are creative, inventive and discoverers."

What is creativity? Ned Herrmann defines it as "a process of becoming sensitive to problems, deficiencies, gaps in knowledge, missing elements and disharmonies; identifying the difficulty, searching for solutions, making guesses, formulating hypotheses about the deficiencies; testing and retesting these hypotheses and possibly modifying and retesting them; and communicating the results." If all this sounds beyond the realm of the preschool or primary child, think again. By sharing Arnold Lobel's *Frog and Toad* stories children will see this process again and again. In *Frog and Toad Together* these two good friends become sensitive to many problems. In the story "Cookies" they decide that if they continue to eat the cookies they will get sick. They then identify the difficulties in *not* eating the cookies which are so readily available. They search for solutions. First they try putting the cookies in a box but discover they can easily open the box. Then they try or test various other solutions . . . putting a string around the box, putting the box on a high shelf . . . nothing works. Finally they *hypothesize* that birds might like the cookies so to test the hypothesis they take the box outside and call for the birds. Sure enough, "Birds came from everywhere. They picked up all the cookies in their beaks and flew away." The problem was solved! "Now we have no more cookies to eat," said Toad sadly as he *communicated* the results to frog.

There are four types of thinking that can lead to creativity and
each of these can be stimulated by
picture books: fluency, originality,
flexibility and elaboration.

Fluency is the ability to make
many responses. A good fluency exercise can come from any picture.

EXAMPLE (right):

This little girl is cleaning up her
backyard. Name all of the things
she might pick up to put in the trash
bag.

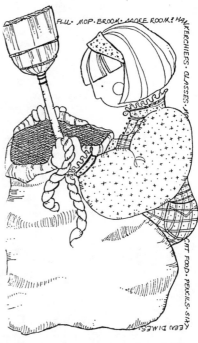

Originality has to do with
unique and unusual responses.
Many children's books are highly
original in nature and can stimulate
original thinking in young minds. In
Joann Ryder's *White Bear, Ice Bear* (William Morrow, 1989) the child is
taken on a fantasy journey from the center of his or her warm, cozy bedroom
to the icy peaks of the frozen North. The author suggests that the child become an ice bear and experience the walk through icy terrains, watching
a seal escape from his
clutches, and finally re-
turning to the familiar
sights and smells of
home. This book is
filled with sensory im-
ages and is the first in a
series designed to stim-
ulate imaginative and
original thought.

EXAMPLE (left):
This is Mrs. Nooter.
What is the most origi-
nal idea you can think of
to tell why she is push-
ing her computer down
the street?

How many original verses can you add to this poem?

EATING
LIZARDS

Billy Izzard
Ate some lizards
Tossed their tails
In garbage pails.
Billy's brother
Ate another
Got in trouble with his mother!
No more lizards
For the Izzards.

TRY

Cynthia Squirm ate a worm

Arthur Lake ate a snake

Sally Rider ate a spider

Flexible thinking has to do with stretching the mind to find new categories, new uses or new ways of doing things.

How many uses can you think of for two jars of honey other than spreading the honey on your biscuit or toast?

Flexibility means findings new categories, or new uses for familiar objects.

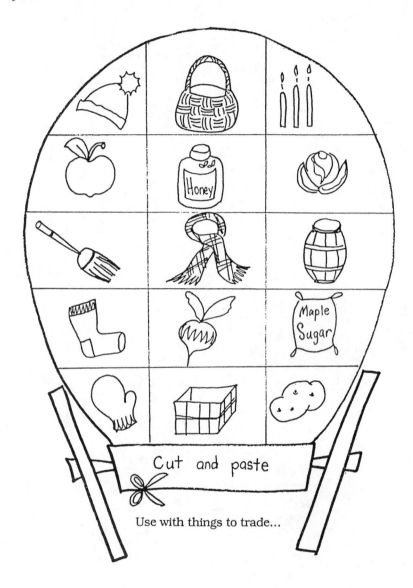

How many different groups of things can you find in this cart? List them on another sheet of paper.

Elaboration is possibly the most difficult of the productive or creative thinking skills. It means adding to a basic product in order to create an original product or idea. Elaboration requires a careful study of the product to be added to in order to bring about change in original and unique ways.

What drawing or words could you add to this picture to make it a funny cartoon?

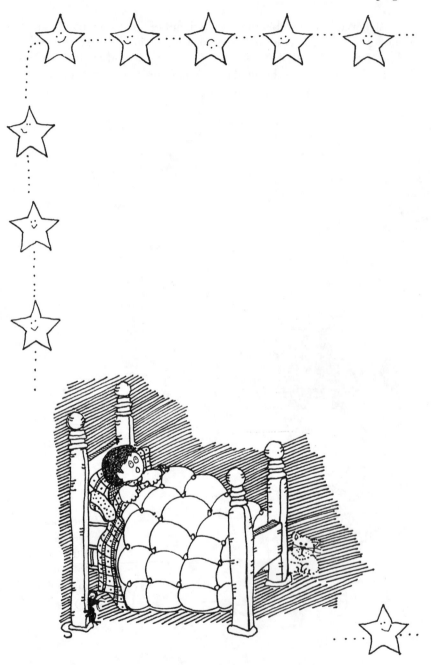

This little boy is imagining that he sees something on the ceiling of his room. Add to the picture the "something" that he sees.

The daily routing of required pursuits tends to squelch the creative spirit. The right books can keep it nurtured and alive. Parents of primary children often ask, "How can I share with my child the easiest primer with any sense of understanding or meaning?" The quickest and surest method is to read aloud. Even if your child is reading, read aloud to him or her daily, not as a parental chore, but because you are so excited about the book that you can't wait to share it! It takes time to find those very special books that demand sharing. But the rewards may be startling! When you build a rapport by sharing exciting, or moving or funny things from literature, a mutual trust between parent and child grows and grows which gives an aura of expectancy to any moment when you reach a book. Exposure through the printed word and magnificent art work of the creators of picture books can stimulate creative thought and action. According to Paul Torrance, "It is possible to teach children to think creatively. Most successes come with a combined cognitive and emotional functioning." This is precisely the kind of experience that can be gained from quality literature.

Among the many fine books that can stimulate creative thought are those by Babette Cole. In *Princess Smartypants* (Putnam, 1987) the Princess is happy being single and does not want to marry any of the princes who seek her hand. Finally at the urging of her parents she states that the prince who can accomplish all of the tasks she sets forth will be the one she will marry. The tasks are both difficult and humorous and no prince is successful until along comes Prince Swashbuckle! He accomplishes each task with ease and now the Princess is faced with creative problem solving! How can she get out of marrying the Prince, yet not go back on her word. The solution is as humorous as the rest of this delightful tale.

Patricia McKissack has her heroine do creative problem-solving in a realistic setting. In *Flossie and the Fox* (Dial, 1987) Flossie has to safely take a basket of eggs through the woods to Miss Viola's house. On the way she meets a fox "who just dearly loves eggs." Flossie solves the problem by refusing to recognize the fox who becomes more and more frustrated trying to convince the little girl that he is indeed a fox. By the time he figures out a way to convince her, a hound dog chases the fox away.

Author Pat Hutchins is well-known for her creative books for preschool and primary children. She shows in *The Doorbell Rang* (Greenwillow, 1986) that young children can think and act creatively when faced with a problem situation. The tale begins with two children and 12 chocolate chip cookies. Each time the doorbell rings more children arrive and the cookies are shared. The last time the doorbell rings there are already 12 children at the table and each has one cookie. Young children get so involved in this tale that they become immediate problem solvers at this point. Ideas range from "Don't answer the door" to "Eat fast!" to "We could break the cookies in half and share."

For slightly older children Steven Manes's *Life Is No Fair* sets up a problem solving situation on one page and creatively solves it on the next. Children have many ideas about what happened to "Willard Twombly who worried that when he moved to a new neighborhood that he would never have another friend." The author's solution to this and other problems in the book is unique and brings a laugh from young readers.

Barbara Williams deals creatively with everyday life in *Albert's Toothache* (Dutton, 1974). Albert the young turtle claims he has a toothache. No one believes him for it is a fact that turtles do not have teeth. Albert, however, cannot be talked out of his toothache and refuses to get out of bed. The solution comes with the arrival of Grandmother who asks Albert, "Where does the tooth ache?" "Here, on my toe," answers Albert. "A gopher bit me and I have a toothache." Grandmother makes things better for Albert and chastizes the rest of the family for not believing him!

A simpler definition of creativity than that given by Ned Herrmann is one developed by James A. Smith. He defines creativity as "the ability to tap past experiences and come up with something new." For parents of preschool primary children the task is to provide experiences that can be tapped and that will stimulate neural growth in the brain's creative quadrant. This can be done through the creative sharing of special picture books. Using any of the books recommended in this chapter the following guidelines will be helpful in talking with your child about the book both during and after the sharing time.

1. Choose books that will contain ideas new to the child.

2. Ask questions about what might happen in the story. Encourage many guesses or possibilities, not just one.

3. Challenge your child to think. If he/she offers only one idea about how Frog and Toad can keep from eating the cookies, and seems satisfied with the one idea, challenge the child to come up with one or two more ideas.

4. Remember that in creative thinking outcomes are not predictable. Often the authors we enjoy and or admire most are those who give us unpredictable endings or solutions to their stories.

5. In sharing books with your child point out areas of special uniqueness or originality.

6. Let your child set his or her own pace with literature. Very young children are never bored with repetition and often want stories read again and again. Very young children will show preferences for a particular page or one part of an illustration. Let them enjoy at their leisure and return again and again to a beloved passage or work of art.

7. Help your child move from being an observer of illustra-

tions in fine books to being an observer of the world around him. Alan Dow in "An Architect's View of Creativity" says, "No matter where we may look, the process of creativity is at work. It may be in the growing of a plant, erosion of a mountain or the swelling of the sea. All is change, all is individual and everywhere is creativeness." (*Creativity and Its Cultivation*, Harper and Row, 1959).

Each time your child meets a new experience whether from literature or real life his or her direct involvement with the experience causes new neural networks to form in the brain. By exposing your child to creative experiences in picture books with ideas that are new and by guiding your child to interact with the literature through solving problems and predicting outcomes as well as through careful observation of the illustrations you will be helping the child to greater brain power.

The books described in the remainder of this chapter are those that in the opinion of this author have unique creative elements. The list is meant as a starting point for identifying particularly creative elements in children's literature and for introducing authors who show exceptional originality in their work.

References

Duckworth, Eleanor. "Piaget Takes a Teacher's Look." *Learning*, Oct. 1973.

Herrmann, Ned. *The Creative Brain*. Applied Creative Services, 1988.

Lobel, Arnold. *Frog and Toad Together*. Harper and Row, 1972.

Polette, Nancy, and Hamlin, Marjorie. *Exploring Books with Gifted Children*. Libraries Unlimited, 1980.

Smith, James A. *Creative Teaching of the Language Arts in the Elementary School*. Prentice-Hall, 1967.

Torrance, E. Paul. *Guiding Creative Talent*. Prentice-Hall, 1962.

Suggested Children's Reading

Creativity

Agee, John. *The Incredible Painting of Felix Clousseau*. Illus. by author. Farrar, Straus and Giroux, 1988. (Ages 4–8).

"Outrageous!" the judges cried. "Ridiculous!" Who would dare enter the portrait of a duck in the Grand Contest of Art? But when Felix Clousseau's painting quacks, he is hailed as a genius. Suddenly everyone wants a Clousseau masterpiece and the unknown painter becomes an overnight sensation. That's when the trouble begins. The volcano painting erupts, the waterfall painting floods the town. Felix is jailed and all of his paintings are seized . . . except one! How that one painting saves the day makes a clever ending to a very unusual and creative story.

Bang, Molly. *Delphine.* Illus. by author. Morrow, 1988. (Ages 4–6).
As sunny as the colorful flowers for which she is named, Delphine lives with three companions—a wolf, a lion and her guinea pig, Joe—in a cabin high on the mountaintop. Then one day she receives a letter from her grandmother. There's a present waiting for her far below at the post office.
Anxious about her ability to handle the mysterious gift, Delphine is unaware of her amazing feats of courage and skill as she journeys down the steep slope, across the narrow bridge, and through treacherous rapids. A wordless picture book that speaks to the everyday concerns of children in a unique way.

Birdseye, Tom. *Airmail to the Moon.* Illus. by Stephen Gammell. Holiday House, 1988. (Ages 4–8).
"My name is Ora Mae Cotton of Crabapple Orchard, and last night somebody stole my tooth . . . somebody so crooked they screw their socks on every morning. And when I catch 'em, I'm gonna open up a can of gotcha and send 'em airmail to the moon!"
Ora Mae is cork-poppin' mad. Somebody took her tooth, and she's high-nigh sure it wasn't the tooth fairy. She goes to Mama, Dadaw, brother Bo Dean and sister Kelsey Ann, but nobody has seen her lost tooth. Ora Mae won't give up until she finds the "lop-eared rascal" who stole it.

Cazet, Denys. *Great Uncle Felix.* Illus. by author. Orchard, 1988. (Ages 3–6).
Sam is a regular rhinoceros. He has a mother and a father, a bicycle and lace-up shoes. What makes him special is his Great Uncle Felix. Today his great-uncle has come down to town for a visit. Sam has made him his all-time most-special invention, a bicycle rack to hold his suitcase. Sam can't wait to show it off.
Great Uncle Felix can't wait to show Sam the special yo-yo he's brought him. But by the time they've left the bus station, crossed the park, circled the lake and reached Sam's house, Great Uncle Felix and Sam have shown each other friendship quite a bit more special.

Cole, Babette. *King Change-a-lot.* Illus. by author. Philomel, 1989. (Ages 4–8).
Prince Change-a-lot thinks his parents are a royal pain in the diaper. They've allowed the kingdom to be overrun by rampaging dragons, beastly blubber worms, and bad fairies cooking up rotten spells. Taking matters into his own hands, the prince rubs his pony and summons a baby genie who not only sees eye to eye with his young highness, but is prepared to lend a hand with some "improvements."

———. *Prince Cinders.* Illus. by author. E.P. Putnam's, 1988. (Ages 5–8).
Poor Prince Cinders—he's small, spotty, scruffy and skinny. His three big hairy brothers tease him about his looks and make him clean the house while they go off to the Palace Disco and dance with princesses. Then one evening, a fairy falls down the chimney and promises to grant Prince Cinders's wishes. She isn't too good at spells, but even so, Prince Cinders attracts the attention of a beautiful princess in a most unexpected way. This is a new twist on an old tale.

———. *Three Cheers for Errol!* Illus. by author. Putnam, 1989. (Ages 4–8).

Errol, the city rat, is always being told how dumb he is. Although he just can't figure out math, spelling or science, he's good at one thing—sports. When he's picked to represent his school in the Ratathalon, Errol's competitors can't stand the idea of a rat from such a scruffy school winning the city-wide athletic contest. They plot to keep him out of the race, but with the aid of his remarkable tail, Errol outwits the competition.

Engel, Diana. *Josephina, the Great Collector*. Illus. by author. Morrow, 1988. (Ages 4–7).

For Josephina, the world is full of treasures just waiting to be seen and held and kept. The trouble is that her collection is taking over the cozy bedroom she shares with her sister Rosie. "Can't you throw some of it out?" Rosie asks about Josephina's special, private collection. Josephina tries leaving selected items with their Uncle Mario, but somehow she only ends up with more. Will she really have to choose between her tidy sister and her beloved junk?

There is a solution and young children will be captivated as Josephina works it out in this warm-hearted story about two loving but very different sisters.

Hollands, Judith. *Mrs. Mudgie and Mr. James*. Illus. by Ned Delaney. Atheneum, 1988. (Ages 4–7).

It isn't fair. Mrs. Mudgie gets tea and black jelly beans and she isn't even real. "That's because she's imaginary," Tabitha tells Timothy. "I made her up in my mind and she's my best friend."

Mrs. Mudgie also makes flags for a living, sings opera, and can shuffle-hop-step while she whistles "Yankee Doodle Dandy" and drinks a glass of water.

"Well, I have an imaginary friend, too," says Timothy. "I made him up in my mind and his name is Mr. James."

Has Mrs. Mudgie met her match? Tabitha certainly has, as she and Timothy engage in a battle of imaginations that gradually transforms their rivalry into friendship.

Kasza, Keiko. *The Pigs' Picnic*. Illus. by author. Putnam's, 1988. (Ages 3–6).

Mr. Pig wants to look his best as he sets out to ask Miss Pig to go on a picnic with him. He gets all kinds of advice from his friends the Fox, the Lion and the Zebra, but when he does what they suggest, the effect on Miss Pig is not at all what he intended. How can he persuade her that a picnic with him would be a perfect way to spend an afternoon?

_____. *The Wolf's Chicken Stew*. Illus. by author. E.P. Putnam's, 1987. (Ages 4–8).

The wolf loves to eat more than anything in the world and one day he has a terrible craving for chicken stew. He spots a chicken who seems just right, but then he thinks how much more stew there would be if he fattened her up before dining. So he goes home and begins to cook all kinds of scrumptious food for the chicken to eat. A big surprise is in store for the wolf when he finally visits Mrs. Chicken to collect his meal.

Koontz, Robin Michal. *Dinosaur Dream*. Illus. by author. E.P. Putnam's, 1988. (Ages 3–6).

Shane is disappointed when it's time to put his dinosaur toys away and go to bed, but his disappointment vanishes when he dreams he is awakened and carried away by a real Apatosaurus.

In his dream, he sees and experiences a world from the past, with dinosaurs and prehistoric creatures of every size, shape and color. The dinosaur world can be a fun place, but danger is always lurking. Shane's dinosaur friend hides him in a tree when the fearsome Tyrannosaurus enters the scene, and he is rescued by a Triceratops that looks a lot like his favorite toy. Finally he finds himself at home in his bed—but was it all a dream?

MacDonald, George. *Little Daylight*. Illus. by Frank Ingraham. Morrow, 1988. (Ages 6–8).
   When little Daylight was born, there was great jubilation in the palace, for this was the queen's first baby. But when seven fairies come to bestow their remarkable gifts on the child, the king and queen never thought of inviting the old hag who lived in the swampy part of the forest. This vengeful fairy casts a terrible spell. Little Daylight will sleep during the day and awake only at night, and her beauty will wax and wane with the cycles of the moon until a prince comes who will kiss her without knowing who she is. This romantic tale has entertained children for more than 100 years and is presented here as a visual feast.

Pinkwater, Daniel. *Aunt Lulu*. Illus. by author. Macmillan, 1988. (Ages 5–8).
   Why are 14 Alaskan huskies sporting sunglasses with pink frames? For one thing, the sun is very bright as they pull their fourwheeled dogsled around the town. Every week Aunt Lulu, librarian, hitches up her dog team and braves the frozen wastes of the North to bring new books to the gold miners who live at the diggings. And every week she brings back the books they've read. Eventually Aunt Lulu decides she needs a change. But where can she go with 14 Alaskan huskies and a dogsled in tow? Why, to Parsippany, New Jersey, of course!
   Children will giggle as each new page reveals the next stage in Aunt Lulu's trip back home to family friends—and warmer weather.

Riddell, Chris. *The Trouble with Elephants*. Illus. by author. Lippincott, 1988. (Ages 3–6).
   What is the trouble with elephants? The little girl in this story knows . . . they rattle the windowpanes at night when they snore, they eat all the cupcakes at picnics and they are not very good at playing hide-and-seek. There are other problems with elephants, too, as children will discover.

Ross, Tony. *I'm Coming to Get You!* Illus. by author. Dial, 1984. (Ages 4–7).
   Deep in outer space there's a hairy, howling bully of a monster with a very big appetite. It's been gobbling up the galaxy planet by planet, and now it's heading for Earth. It's coming to get little Tommy Brown! Tommy's heard about monsters and he sure doesn't want to meet any. But tomorrow morning the meanest and hungriest one in the universe will be hiding outside his front door and waiting. . . . All turns out well however, as a huge monster on a tiny planet can be a very tiny monster, indeed, on a huge planet!

————. *Lazy Jack*. Illus. by author. Dial, 1985. (Ages 5–8).
   Jack was the laziest person in the whole world until his mother gave him some advice: "Go out and get a job! Otherwise no more meals from me!" So Jack gets moving and earns a gold coin that he loses on his way home. "Dodo," cries Jack's mom. "You should have put it in your pocket." Trying to please, Jack stashes away his next day's wages. Alas, a pocket is not the best place for a jug of milk.

Then one day, carrying his pay on his back just like Mom said, Jack lumbers home with a donkey. Nearby, a princess whose parents will give anything to see her laugh is moping. Are Jack's fortunes about to change at last in this modern treatment of an old tale?

_____. *Stone Soup.* Illus. by author. Dial, 1987. (Ages 5–7).
What would you do if you were a hen and the Big, Bad Wolf told you he was going to eat you up? Well you could offer him some stone soup the way Mother Hen did. How could any wolf refuse?
"Stone soup is a very special treat," Mother Hen told the wolf, and so easy to fix. All you need to do is boil one stone. Just add salt and pepper and maybe a few carrots to help the stone to cook. And add some barley for balance, and don't forget the potatoes . . . and mushrooms . . . and later on some lentils.
Good food takes time. While the Big, Bad Wolf is waiting, he may be obliging enough to vacuum the house and take in the wash and fix the TV antenna. But what an appetite he'll have when—and if—the delectable soup is finally ready!

_____. *Super, Dooper Jezebel.* Illus. by author. Farrar, Straus and Giroux, 1988. (Ages 5–8).
Jezebel is perfect in every way. She never gets dirty when she goes outside to play. She cleans her room every day, and when she's sick, she takes her medicine without complaining. She even says, "thank you." She's so perfect she's called Super, Dooper Jezebel. But sometimes perfect isn't good enough, and Jezebel is in for a Super Dooper shock!

Rylant, Cynthis. *All I See.* Illus. by Peter Catalanotto. Orchard, 1988. (Ages 4–8).
Charlie stayed hidden in the shadows on shore. The painter, Gregory, drifted beneath the blue sky in a canoe, his white cat curled on his chest, both dreaming. Charlie decided he was fond of Gregory, and once he'd crept from his hiding place and seen all that Gregory saw and painted by their lake, Charlie liked Gregory even better—and could finally say so. This is an unusual story about friendship, about seeing and about sensibility.

Sutherland, Harry A. *Dad's Car Wash.* Illus. by Maxine Chambliss. Atheneum, 1988. (Ages 4–7).
"John played hard all day with his cars and trucks. Boy did he get dirty! When evening came it was time to visit Dad's Car Wash."
John and his father went inside and Dad helped John undress and climb into the tub. Dad scrubbed John's wheels (feet) and hubcaps (knees). he removed the tree sap from John's roof, washed his hood ornament and cleaned out the turn signals. When John was all clean he was newly painted, refueled and parked in the garage for the night. This is a warm and satisfying bedtime story sure to capture the imagination of all small drivers and mechanics and their parents.

Tresselt, Alvin. *Hide and Seek Fog.* Illus. by Roger Duvoisin. Lothrop, Lee and Shepard, 1965. (Ages 3–6).
The worst fog in 20 years rolls in and clouds the seaside village. The boats head back to shore, the sea birds return to their roosts and the people pack up and leave the beach. For three days everyone waits impatiently for the fog to lift. But the children love it, playing hide and seek on the rocks and getting lost in front of their own cottages.

Wells, Rosemary. *Forest of Dreams.* Illus. by Susan Jeffers. Dial, 1988. (Ages 3–6).

This book invites the dreamer in everyone to share in a celebration of the coming of spring. Deep beneath the blanketing snow the earth is sleeping peacefully. But any child can sense the ice melting and revel in nature's dreams of summer — the expectant mother doe; a bird singing from an icy, glistening pine branch; field mice stirring in their burrows. As the days grow longer and snow yields to sifting rain and then to warm sunshine, look and listen as a young girl rejoices with all of nature's children at the return of spring.

Yeoman, John. *Our Village.* Illus. by Quentin Blake. Atheneum, 1988. (Ages 4–7).
      Come and join us in a journey back through time and we will show you what our village used to be like years and years and years ago.

> From the early springtime morning
> Through to moonlight in the snow,
> Past the pond, the school, the baker's,
> Past the blacksmith's fiery glow,
> Stroll with us around our village;
> Meet the people; get to know
> How they lived and walked and played there
> Years and years and years ago.

Here is a visual and poetic journey to another age and time filled with details from the past.

Yorinks, Arthur. *Bravo Minski.* Illus. by Richard Egielski. Farrar, Straus and Giroux, 1988. (Ages 4–8).
      The greatest scientist who ever lived? The name synonymous with *genius*? It's Minski, of course.
      Minski is barely three when he proves the theory of gravity. At seven he discovers electricity. What a marvel! So his proud papa packs their bags and sets off across Europe to show the world his remarkable son. London, Paris, Vienna . . . new inventions from rocket ships to aspirin, just pour out of Minski. Naturally, he's showered with acclaim. But wait! Is wonderful, brilliant success enough for him?
      No. In Rome, Minski is inspired to reach for the ultimate scientific achievement. And with perseverance and singular vision, he triumphantly accomplishes the impossible . . . to become the world's greatest singer!

6

Books to Touch the Heart

Books that are worth reading at all are bursting with the major passions which concern us all. Love, hate, fear, superstition, remorse, compassion, tenderness come to life under the pen of an inspired writer. Great works of art bring forth responses in all of us as they touch our deepest instincts, our determination for justice and truth. What child could not feel the compassion for the birds of the night as the "owl man" heals their injured wings in *The Man Who Could Call Down Owls* by Eve Bunting. It is a rare child who will not both laugh and cry with the Bunyip as he seeks his identity in *The Bunyip of Berkley's Creek* by Jenny Wagner.

In experiences over the years at the Laboratory School of Lindenwood College, this author has met many concerned parents who want only the best for their child . . . intellectually. To many anxious parents of preschoolers, the child who is not reading well by age five is labeled a failure. These parents are overly concerned with the skill and drill that they see as intellectual development and feed their children a steady diet of fact books . . . from astronomy to paleontology. These truly caring parents need to be helped to understand that this child needs books to touch the heart and to help his humanity keep pace with his intellect. Exposure to fine literature can help the heart to sing along with the mind!

For example, a child could not help but be enthralled by the realistic, very human story of *The Biggest Bear* by Lynd Ward. The problems in this story have no easy solutions. Johnny dearly loves the bear he has raised from a cub. The bear is destroying the needed food stores of Johnny's family and of the neighbors who to have food for the winter, will have to kill the bear if its foraging is not stopped. Taking the bear into the woods is not effective. The bear always returns. Is there no way to save the bear *and* the family's winter food supply?

It is often helpful to lure highly intellectual children to a realistic problem-solving story first rather than make-believe worlds. The child should be given time to think about the problem and to suggest more than one idea for solving the problem. Stories like *The Biggest Bear* can be very effective

in helping children walk in another's shoes, share laughter and tears of
another and wrestle with problems that are not easy to solve.

The story is described here:

The Biggest Bear is the story of Johnny who lives on a farm farthest up
the valley and closest to the woods. But Johnny's barn is the only barn in
the valley without a bearskin nailed up to dry. Johnny decides to do something about this humiliating situation and goes looking for the biggest bear
in the woods. Instead of a big bear, Johnny finds a cub. Soon the cub grows
into a big bear which eats Johnny's maple sugar, the family's food and the
neighboring farmer's corn, hams and maple syrup. Johnny's father said the
bear must go.

Johnny loves the bear, and the bear loves Johnny. The bear does not
want to go back to the woods. Each time, the bear returns. Johnny and the
big bear are in big trouble. Finally Johnny takes the bear to the farthest part
of the woods. The bear takes off in the direction of his favorite smell, maple

sugar. The bear is trapped and taken to a zoo where Johnny visits regularly, always bringing maple sugar for his big bear.

Yesterday's bright children of technology have taken us outward to the moon — but have we traveled far enough to find our own hearts? Yesterday's young intellectuals have built nuclear power plants — but have we found the power which reinforces all life? Yesterday's quiz kids have constructed bridges spanning the waters between nations — but have we bridged the chasms which prejudice and bigotry have dug amongst the family of man? Can we afford *not* to take the time to share literature which will reach the spirit of a potentially great thinker?

If literature can help our children grow in compassion and understanding (those qualities of thinking developed in the lower right brain quadrant), it is worth every effort, including putting off dishes while the family is still gathered together in a captive, read-aloud audience.

Albert Einestein in *The Human Side* says:

> Humanity has every reason to place the proclaimers of high moral standards and values above the discoverer of objective truth. What humanity owes to personalities like Buddha, Moses and Jesus ranks for me higher than all the achievements of the enquiring, constructive mind.

One of the master "proclaimers of standards and values" was the late Arnold Lobel. His creation of the four *Frog and Toad* books — collections of short, short tales for beginning readers — is filled with subtle, yet powerful messages of the value of friendship, the obligatons that accompany caring for another person, the value of reading and of books, and the value of simple pleasures. Frog and Toad are not found in the video game parlor, or the local amusement park. Theirs is a celebration of nature and of man's humanity to man.

Young children revel in the absurd, which is one reason these books are so popular. In the story of "The Hat" from *Days with Frog and Toad,* Toad's hat is too big. He tries to solve the problem by thinking big thoughts to make his head grow larger. In "Spring," Frog is tired of winter and wants spring to come. His father tells him that "spring is just around the corner," so Frog goes out to look for that corner. His search is unsuccessful until at last he arrives home, tired and hungry, and goes around the corner of his house. There he finds spring . . . birds singing, his father and mother working in the garden and a warm sun.

People tend to act on the covert message not the overt message. We can say to children, "Be kind, be truthful, be loving." There is little power in this kind of overt admonition. Frog and Toad, however, *are* kind and loving and truthful. They enjoy life and each other. The covert message is clear and will not be lost on a child as a parent reads aloud these tales and parent

and child together try to solve the simple, everyday problems these two friends meet.

Children's books abound with themes dealing with life's stresses and losses. Exposure to these books can help the child identify with a character and experience the same wide range of emotions the character experiences as life's losses are confronted. Every good story contains conflict. As the child lives through literature, the ways in which others meet and deal with adversity, compassion and feeling begin to develop. Consider these books as "inoculations" which will eventually enable the child to examine values and to make judgments and decisions for his or her own life.

A fine example of a children's book that deals with loss is Kay Chorao's *Cathedral Mouse* (E.P. Dutton, 1988).

Mouse has always wanted a real home. But when he slips out of the pet store, he discovers that a safe place for a small mouse is not easy to find. To escape a cat he scurries up broad stone steps . . . into a vast and mysterious space.

Mouse is in a cathedral, and he soon finds it is full of wonders. Sunlight streams through the jewel-like windows. Intricate carvings cover walls and pillars . . . so many beautiful things to see, and so much fun for him to explore.

But the cathedral doesn't have a home for Mouse until he makes a very special friend. His friend's kindness and unique talent result in the perfect home for Mouse—not just a place, but something created by love.

Two- and three-year-olds understand the need for a warm, loving place in which they feel safe. Losing that place can be scary. But when love comes in another form and Mouse finds once again a warm, cozy, safe place to live, little children breathe a sigh of relief and the first seeds of compassion are sewn.

It is Lloyd Alexander's deep concern about the lack of individual commitment in our lives today that led him to create (for primary children) the beautiful story, *The King's Fountain* (Dutton, 1971). Ezra Jack Keats caught the humility and apparent helplessness of the poor peasant poignantly in his magnificent illustrations. He contrasted the qualities of character as vividly in paint as Lloyd Alexander had done with words. The message is clear and alive: if only *one* will stand, that will be enough. Suggestions bombard us all to indicate that we are not that one. But it is in the heart of the simplest and least of us to be that one. The peasant's child in this story had the pure faith to give her father the needed courage which saved their village. What a lesson in trust, perseverance and triumph.

It is important to note the contrast in these two equally beautiful books. *Cathedral Mouse* sets forth a problem that very young children will understand. The warm, safe nest and loving parents are the young child's world. Risking one's life for others as the peasant does in *The King's Fountain* is beyond the understanding of the very young child. Indeed, preschoolers, because of their naturally immature neurological systems, may find humor in tragedy. In choosing books to touch the hearts of very young children the setting must be that of home and family, either animal or human. As the child enters kindergarten and moves through the primary grades the range of literature can be expanded—settings in other cultures and losses of a more abstract nature, loss of friendship or self-esteem.

Probably the most famous tale ever written about finding one's place in the world is Hans Christian Andersen's *Ugly Duckling*. Every child will be rejected by someone at some time. Every child, too, is a priceless being and must come to believe in his or her self worth. After sharing this story, discuss each event with your child as he or she recalls and places each event in its correct sequence. A simple story? Yes. But it is a strong lesson in humanity.

Consider for a moment the bill parents pay for using television rather than literature to capture the child's attention. Watch the typical Saturday morning cartoons. What is the level of language used? Simple or complex? How are problems solved. Through violence or through reasoned dialogue? How much time is the child given to observe a visual before it is replaced by another? Could there be a connection between the rapid changes of visuals and subjects on television and the growing number of primary teachers reporting children with attention deficit disorder? What real human feeling is the child getting from the television cartoon? Is the bill too high?

The list of books written to touch the heart (or more precisely, the lower right brain quadrant) is a long one, and it would be impossible to compile a list that purports to suggest the best of these titles. The list that follows is not intended to be a "best" list, but instead a representative list of the kinds of books that are available. Books included are relatively recent titles along with several award-winning titles. In searching for other titles to share with your child, the help of your school librarian or of the children's librarian at the public library can be invaluable.

References

Bernhardt, Edythe. *ABCs of Thinking with Caldecott Books*. Book Lures, 1988.
Polette, Nancy. *The Book Report Book for Primary Grades*. Book Lures, 1979 (Ugly Duckling Activity).
Polette, Nancy, and Hamlin, Marjorie. *Exploring Books with Gifted Children*. Libraries Unlimited, 1980.

Suggested Children's Reading

Abolafia, Yossi. *A Fish for Mrs. Gardenia*. Illus. by author. Greenwillow, 1988. (Ages 4–7).

When Mr. Bennett caught the big fish, he invited Mrs. Gardenia to come for dinner and share it with him. But while he was preparing it, the fish slipped from his hands and shot into Mrs. Murgle's apartment. She shrieked and threw it out the window. And that was the beginning of a hilarious misadventure with the happiest of endings. If you can stop laughing long enough, you will find out how fish becomes chicken, chicken becomes fish and Mrs. Gardenia becomes Mrs. Bennett.

Alexander, Lloyd. *The King's Fountain.* Illus. by Ezra Jack Keats. E.P. Dutton, 1971. (Ages 4–8).

Blaustein, Muriel. *Play Ball, Zachary!* Illus. by author. Harper and Row, 1988. (Ages 4–7).

Zachary, the tiger cub, and his father, Mr. Tiger, want to do things together. Zachary is good at counting, reading, painting and doing jigsaw puzzles. His dad wants him to play baseball, football and basketball. Even though Zachary tries his best, they are both disappointed with the results. Zachary is *not* good at playing ball.

In this second warm and funny story about the irrepressible tiger cub of *Bedtime, Zachary!*, Muriel Blaustein presents a delightful, loving solution to a familiar problem.

Boholm-Olsson, Eva. *Tuan.* Illus. by Pham Van Don. R and S Books, 1988. (Ages 5–8).

Tuan's day starts just like most days. The cock crows, the sun rises above the rice fields and Tuan's mother, Mai, hurries him out of bed because she's late for work. While Tuan is visiting his grandmother, a strange dog bites him. Mai is afraid the dog may have rabies, so she rushes Tuan off to the hospital. But medicine is scarce in Vietnam. Will the doctor be able to get the serum that will prevent Tuan from getting sick? Luckily, he does, and once again Tuan and Mai can celebrate the Children's Festival together.

Boujon, Claude. *The Cross-Eyed Rabbit.* Illus. by author. McElderry, 1988. (Ages 3–6).

Three rabbits, who are brothers, live in a burrow in the woods. Two are always together. One stays alone. He is cross-eyed, and his brothers never stop teasing him about it. "Look to the right to see to the left. Look up to see down. Ah-ha-ha, ah-ha-ha!" they keep chanting. But he says nothing. Instead, he stays in the burrow and writes poems.

Then one night, a hungry fox comes to the woods. Rabbit is his favorite food, and when he smells the two brothers close by he knows he will soon have a splendid meal. But as he is creeping low to the ground to catch them, a blade of grass tickles his nose and he sneezes. Away go the rabbits and they are sure the fox will never catch up with them. Yet closer and closer he comes. Their only chance of survival, at last, is to get back to their burrow but the fox gets there first and blocks the entrance with his bushy tail.

The surprise ending — in which the cross-eyed rabbit's odd vision saves the day — is a happy climax to this funny-scary (but not too) story that, with its childlike, full-color pictures, will delight the young.

Choaro, Kay. *Cathedral Mouse.* E.P. Dutton, 1988. (Ages 4–8).

Cohen, Miriam. *See You Tomorrow, Charles.* Illus. by Lillian Hoban. Greenwillow, 1983. (Ages 4–7).

Charles is a new boy in class, and he is blind. "You better not punch Charles!" Anna Maria says to Danny, who is a prizefighter. "Yes, because he can't see who is punching him," George adds. After three weeks first grade still doesn't quite know what to do, or the right things to say to Charles. But the time comes when they learn that Charles is their peer, and that there are things he can do even better than they can.

Miriam Cohen guides first grade through another important experience, and her lesson, as always, is wise, gentle and thoroughly satisfying.

de Paola, Tomie. *The Art Lesson.* Illus. by author. Philomel, 1989. (Ages 4–8).
Tommy knows he wants to be an artist when he grows up. He can't wait to start school and have real art lessons with Mrs. Bowers, who wears a blue smock and carries a box of colored chalks into the classroom. But Tommy is surprised and dismayed when he gets to school and finds out there are "rules" to follow. Worst of all, instead of creating his own picture from his imagination, he's expected to copy Mrs. Bower's drawing and he knows that *real* artists don't copy. How this wise art teacher finds a way to give Tommy the freedom to create and stay within the rules makes a wonderfully perceptive picture book about growing up and keeping one's individuality.

Homelund, Else. *Little Bear.* Illus. by Maurice Sendak. Harper and Row, 1957. (Ages 4–8).
Meet Little Bera, a friend to millions of children. And meet Mother Bear, who is there whenever Little Bear needs her. When it is cold and snowy outside, she finds just the right outfit for Little Bear to play in. When he goes to the moon, she has a hot lunch waiting for him on his return. At night she helps him get to sleep. And, of course, she never forgets his birthday.

Joosse, Barbara M. *Better with Two.* Illus. by Catherine Stock. Harper and Row, 1988. (Ages 4–8).
Every morning, while Laura rides her bike, Mrs. Brady and Max take a walk. They walk slowly, because Max is very old. Afterward they have tea and sit on the porch swing listening to the radio. Sometimes they sing. Max likes "I've Been Working on the Railroad" best. On special days Laura joins them.
Then one day Max dies. Now Mrs. Brady sits on the porch swing alone. The swing does not work well with one. Every day Laura brings Mrs. Brady a special present, but still Mrs. Brady looks sad. Finally Laura remembers crying and hugging with Mama and rushes back to Mrs. Brady.

Keller, Holly. *Geraldine's Blanket.* Illus. by author. Mulberry, 1984. (Ages 3–5).
Geraldine loves her baby blanket. Trouble is, she's not a baby anymore—and neither is her blanket. It may be old and tattered, but Geraldine won't get rid of it, much to her parents' dismay. "It looks silly," says her mother. "There's hardly any blanket left," says her father. But when Aunt Bessie sends her a new doll for Christmas, Geraldine thinks of a solution that makes everybody happy.

Lobel, Arnold. *Days with Frog and Toad.* Harper and Row, 1972. (Ages 3–6).

McKissack, Patricia. *Mirandy and Brother Wind.* Illus. by Jerry Pinkney. Knopf, 1988. (Ages 6–8).
Tomorrow night is Mirandy's first cakewalk, and somehow, some way, she's going to be kicking up her heels with Brother Wind!
But how do you catch the Wind? Grandmama Beasley says, "Can't nobody put shackles on Brother Wind, chile. He be special. He be free." With neighbors up and down Ridgetop suggesting all manner of strategies, and friend Ezel laughing at each foiled one, Mirandy grows ever more determined. She'll get hold of that Brother Wind yet!
Patricia C. McKissack's thoroughly engaging tale dances with spirit and rollick-

ing good humor. Complemented by Jerry Pinkney's rich, eye-catching watercolors of the rural South, here's one of those rare rewarding picture books that is sure to be read and enjoyed again and again.

Miller, Montzalee. *My Grandmother's Cookie Jar.* Illus. by Katherine Potter. Price/Stern/Sloan, 1987. (Ages 5–8).
  The stories passed from generation to generation keep family histories alive. In this touching tale, Grandmother captures her grandchild's imagination and calms her fears by sharing stories of Indian life long ago. But one day Grandmother is no longer there. Grandfather helps the little girl see that Grandmother's cookie jar will always remain full of her love because the child will share the gifts of their heritage with her own little ones someday.

Rice, Eve. *Aren't You Coming Too?* Illus. by Nancy Winslow Parker. Greenwillow, 1988. (Ages 3–5).
  Everyone has somewhere to go. Lily is off to school. Mama and Papa go to work. The paperboy delivers his papers. Even Willy the dog seems to ask, "Aren't you coming too?" as he walks by. But Amy has nowhere to go—that is, until Grandpa arrives. Then off they go, for a wonderful adventure of their own.

Shles, Larry. *Hoots and Toots and Hairy Brutes.* Illus. by author. Houghton Mifflin, 1985. (Ages 5–9).
  In *Hoots and Toots and Hairy Brutes,* Squib—who can only toot—determines to overcome this handicap by setting out to learn how to give a mighty hoot. His own attempts result in abject failure. Then his mother tries to straighten him out by sending him to a series of specialists. Alas, all attempts to bring out Squib's hoot are for naught. He's doomed to toot his life away. Then, in a do-or-die crisis, Squib discovers an amazing fact about his life—his toot was everything he ever really needed.
  Every reader who has struggled with life's limitations will recognize his own struggles and triumphs in the microcosm of Squib's forest world for in Squib we find a parable for all ages.

————. *Moths and Mothers, Feathers and Fathers.* Houghton Mifflin, 1984. (Ages 4–8).

Steig, William. *Spinky Sulks.* Illus. by author. Farrar, Straus and Giroux, 1988. (Ages 4–6).
  Spinky's awful family! They don't love him, they don't understand him, and nothing any of them can say or do will convince him otherwise. Not his mother's kisses and crullers, not his father's reasonable lecture, not the visits of sister, brother, grandma and friends. The world was against him, so he was against the world, and that included all living things—except, of course, the animals. What can Spinky possibly do but lie in his hammock "like a pile of laundry," with a blinding case of the sulks? And what can his loving, patient family do to help him out of it?
  William Steig addresses himself to this problem with his usual wit and vigor. In Spinky Sulks, Steig's storytelling is at its most playful, with dazzling illustrations to match.

Stevenson, Sucie. *I Forgot.* Illus. by author. Orchard, 1988. (Ages 4–7).
  Try as he may, Arthur Peter Platypus, Jr., can't get the hang of remembering details such as whether today is a school day, the names of the oceans or the answer to 2 plus 2.
  He thinks of tying strings to his flippers. He tries writing himself reminder

notes by the pile. Nothing works. Arthur's memory works best when the day is not a detail, but important.

Udry, Janice May. *Let's Be Enemies.* Illus. by author. Harper and Row, 1961. (Ages 3–6).

James used to be my friend. But today he is my enemy.

James and John are best frinds — or at least they used to be. They shared pretzels, umbrellas and even chicken pox. Now James always wants to be boss, and John doesn't want to be friends anymore. But when he goes to James's house to tell him so, something unexpected happens.

Vincent, Gabrielle. *Feel Better, Ernest!* Illus. by author. Greenwillow, 1988. (Ages 3–6).

A cold? The flu? Whatever it is, Ernest has caught it. The doctor says he must stay in bed. But with Celestine's excellent care (and entertainment), Ernest is soon well again. And he and his small nurse know just how to celebrate his recovery.

Ward, Lynd. *The Biggest Bear.* Houghton-Mifflin, 1952.

Watts, Bernadette. *St. Francis and the Proud Crow.* Illus. by author. Orchard, 1982. (Ages 4–7).

Crow is envious of Canary's golden cage and asks St. Francis to give him a cage too, so that all can see what a fine bird he is. The kindly saint obliges, but Crow is soon dissatisfied with his new home, for he finds he hasn't room to stretch his wings and fly. How the proud bird eventually learns the value of freedom, with the loving help of a humble little sparrow, is a wise and appealing story which has enchanted children for generations.

Williams, Vera B. *Music, Music for Everyone.* Illus. by author. Mulberry, 1984. (Ages 4–8).

Rosa's Grandma is sick in bed, and the big chair in the living room is usually empty now. So is the family's money jar. Rosa is worried. How can she help?

One thing that makes Grandma feel better is hearing Rosa play music with her friends. She says it makes her feel like a girl again, dancing at a party. This gives Rosa an idea. If Grandma loves their music, maybe people would pay to hear them. That's the beginning of the Oak Street Band.

Winthrop, Elizabeth. *Bear and Mrs. Duck.* Illus. by Patience Brewster. Holiday House, 1988. (Ages 4–7).

Nora loves Bear. They eat lunch together. They read stories together. They sleep in beds right next to each other. One day, Nora has to leave Bear and go to the store. Bear is sick with a cold. He has to stay inside. So Mrs. Duck comes to babysit. Bear does not like Mrs. Duck. He does not want to play or read a story. He only wants to wait for Nora.

Bear soon discovers that waiting is very boring, and that maybe he can have fun with Mrs. Duck.

7

Developing Critical Thinking Abilities

Teaching critical thinking can begin in early childhood. In his delight-ful, yet very simple tale, *Fix-It* (Dutton, 1984), David McPhail shows Emma Bear getting up early one morning to watch television. But the TV wouldn't work, no matter what anyone did. Emma becomes more and more dis-tressed.

In every critical thinking model the first step is to define the problem that needs a solution. Later three-year-olds and four-year-olds have no prob-lem in identifying Emma's problem based on the facts that are given. Her television won't work and she wants to watch it. The second step in the pro-cess is to gather all of the facts about the problem. Again, young children will say that both mother and father and the TV repairman tried to fix it but could not. The third step asks what Emma might do to solve her problem. This is the step that calls for many possibilities, not just one. Young children will reply that she could (1) get mad, (2) cry, (3) get a new TV set, or (4) do something else instead of watching TV. Critical thinking comes into play in selecting the best solution from the list. Which solution chosen is not as important as *why* the child makes a particular choice. In talking about the good and bad points of each option (critical thinking) children can be made aware of the reasons for their choices. Finally the child can hear the solution to the problem the author uses and decide whether or not it was a good solu-tion.

The above steps in critical thinking and problem solving are used in industry to solve major problems, in college and university classes in teach-ing critical thinking and by individuals who show preference for using both the upper and lower left brain quadrants. This kind of experience in early childhood can stimulate neural growth in both the upper and lower left brain quadrants . . . those that control verbal, analytical, sequential, logi-cal thought. But note that at one point in the process the upper right quad-rant was called into play . . . suggesting many possibilities for solving the problem. The lower right quadrant interacts when the young child states how he or she *feels* about Emma's plight. Critical thinking is, then, as are most mental operations, a whole-brain process.

Crosby Bonsall, in her series of beginning readers for four- through eight-year-olds, involves the reader or listener in many critical thinking excursions. The children in her stories often face problems other children will face. They have to plan, predict cause and effect, make decisions, solve problems and evaluate situations before deciding on the best action to take. These charming stories can be read aloud and talked about with very young children and become challenging experiences in critical thinking for the beginning reader. The pages that follow define several critical thinking skills and show how these are found in the Bonsall books.

Critical Thinking Skills

Planning

Planning is determining the steps to be taken in a task, the materials needed and the problems which might be encountered.

In *Mine's the Best*, two boys spend a day on the beach. After sharing this book, children can plan a picnic by making a list of what they will do, the food and equipment they will need, the means of transportation and the picnic place as well as the order in which things must be done.

Forecasting

In *Mine's the Best*, two boys argue over who has the best beach toy. Both toys look alike. Children can be asked to list reasons why an argument might take place over who has the best toy as well as listing causes and effects of arguing with a friend or a brother or sister.

Decision Making

In *The Case of the Scaredy Cats*, Marigod is angry because the boys have decided not to let girls into their club. What reasons did the boys give for this decision? Were they good reasons? Suppose you decided to have a club that anyone could join who wished to. What would be the reasons for allowing anyone to join?

Problem Solving

Problem solving involves the ability to define a problem, determine alternative courses of action, establish criteria for selecting the best alternative, rate the alternatives and plan how to convince others to try your solution.

In *The Case of the Dumb Bells,* by Crosby Bonsall, the boys are in trouble because their parents think the boys are running around the neighborhood ringing doorbells. How can the boys show their parents that they are not guilty? Think of several things they can do. Consider which would be best to try. If one boy does not want to try the solution, how can the others convince him to give it a try?

Predictive Questioning

Predictive questioning is the natural way to approach literature. The typical adult does not finish a novel and then proceed to ask questions about who was in the story or where the story took place. These questions come before reading, not after. It is the anticipation and guessing what will happen next that keeps the reader reading. Yet often in an academic setting children are asked "one right answer" questions after they have read the selection . . . a totally unnatural process.

Note what the work of major researchers has to say about predictive reading:

> Asking predictive questions for reading leads to growth in critical reading and critical thinking abilities.—D. Donlan, "How to Play 29 Questions." *Journal of Reading* 21(6) 535–41, 1978.

> Placement of questions effects what is retained by the reader. If students are to interrelate information and derive generalizations, then *prequestions* that require an interpretative level of response are essential.— R.T. Vacca. *Content Area Reading.* Little, Brown, 1981.

> Good thinkers and readers are good predictors. The proficient reader uses the least amount of information to make the best possible guesses.— K.S. Goodman. "A Psycholinguistic Guessing Game." In H.S. Singer, Ed. *Theoretical Models and Processes of Reading.* IRA, 1970.

> Accurate predictions and reading ability go hand in hand.—J.G. Greeno. "Time to Read Semantically Related Sentences." *Memory and Cognition* 2(1A), 1974.

In reading aloud and talking about books you can help the child to develop critical thinking skills by the questions you ask. Questions like "What do you think will happen next?" (forecasting), "Is there a problem? What do you think it is?" (Problem definition), "How do you think the story will end?" (Suggesting alternative solutions), "How would you solve the problem?" (Problem solving), "If the dog in the story were a cat would the story be different?" (Reorganization), "How is this story like another story we have read?" (Analysis) could be asked. Whatever questions you use, they should arise naturally from the story and be kept to a minimum. One question might be well sufficient to stimulate the child's critical thinking ability.

It is important to note that close observation and the ability to analyze a situation or problem go hand-in-hand. Because the images on television change rapidly, children have little experience with close observation unless encouraged by a wise parent. Picture books can provide this kind of experience. Allow your child ample time to study the illustrations before responding to critical thinking questions. In a fine picture book the illustrations add to the text; they do not simply duplicate the text. The child may well find some person or object in an illustration that can be used in a problem-solving situation that is never mentioned in the text.

Since every story (not every book) is a problem-solving situation, there are literally thousands of choices of picture books to make that will stimulate critical thinking. Many of the Caldecott Award books are ideal for this use, in addition to having award-winning illustrations.

In Arlene Mosel's *The Funny Little Woman*, illustrated by Blair Lent (Dutton, 1972), a little woman in Old Japan who liked to make dumplings out of rice and who liked to laugh spotted a dumpling rolling through a hole in her floor. When she tried to catch it she found herself on a strange road underneath the earth. There, the statues of the gods tried to hide the little woman from the wicked oni. But the oni caught her. The little woman cooked for the oni using a paddle which turned one grain of rice into a potful. Then she became lonesome and tried to run away. What a wonderful book for stirring imagination, predicting what will happen and thinking of many ways to solve the little woman's problem.

From our work with pre-school children in the Laboratory School at Lindenwood College we have discovered that children as young as three and one-half or four can deal with such sophisticated thinking processes as analogy, evaluation, generalizations and solving logic puzzles if stimulated by a good book and guided by a caring adult. Four examples of these types of activities are included here.

Logic Puzzle

In Jane Yolen's *Commander Toad and the Dis-Asteroid* (Coward-McCann, 1985) the crew of Star Warts enjoys an off duty swim. Read the clues or listen carefully to the clues. Study the picture. Can you name each crew member?

CLUES:
1. Jake Skywalker loves to read.
2. Jake Skywalker is between Mr. Hop and Commander Toad.
3. Commander Toad is following Doc Peeper.
4. Lieutenant Lily is following Mr. Hop.

ANSWERS: Clockwise from frog with book: Jake, Commander Toad, Doc Peeper, Lt. Lily, Mr. Hop

Analogy

Mei Li is a little Chinese girl who went to the New Year's Fair in the city. As she walked through the courtyard, she wished a happy New Year to her ducks and pigs. Her small white dog and her thrush went along. At the Fair, Mei Li saw many other animals. See if you can find the missing animals below. Choose the correct animal, cut it out and paste it in the empty box.

Chinese Cut-Up

Generalize

WHAT IS AN ISLAND?

What makes an island? Can you
find islands on your classroom map?
What else can you call an island? What generalization can you
make about islands?

Evaluation

Virginia Lee Burton wrote and illustrated THE LITTLE HOUSE which tells the story about a little house that watches the country turn into a city right before her eyes. Where do you think the Little House wants to live: the country or the city?

1) List the Yes and No reasons for living in the country.

Yes	No

2) Give Yes and No reasons for living in the city.

Yes	No

Where do you think the Little House should live? Read THE LITTLE HOUSE to find out where she wanted to live.

Another enduring classic by Virginia Lee Burton presents several problems needing solutions. In *Mike Mulligan and His Steam Shovel* by Virginia Lee Burton (Houghton Mifflin, 1967), both Mike and the steam shovel, Mary Ann, find their services no longer needed. Mike is jobless. Who might have a need for a steam shovel? After looking at the pictures to gain an understanding of the job of a steam shovel, ask children who might need Mike and Mary Ann to work for them? Mike does get a new job. If he and Mary Ann can dig the cellar for the town hall in one day they will be paid. If they cannot finish in a day they will not be paid. By sundown the job is finished but Mike forgot to leave a way out of the hole! What will he do?

Job Success

Much of Paul Torrance's work showed that there was no relationship between students' high academic performance in college and success in a job after graduation. While these bright students were capable of retaining and giving back knowledge they were unable to solve problems or to think of new ideas on their own . . . skills highly valued by most employers! These students were products of the "one right answer" system of education. Because they were never given the opportunity to examine many alternatives in a situation and to critically assess solutions, these students may well lack those neural connections which as adults they need for success!

The time to develop flexible minds is in early childhood and the primary grades. Lacking our current knowledge of how the human brain works, John Dewey nevertheless made this statement over 50 years ago: "All science is already poetry; we pull against the firmly entrenched nostalgic music of myth and magic. When science shall have cooperated with the course of events and made clear and coherent the meaning of the daily detail, then science and emotion will inner-penetrate practice and imagination will embrace, poetry and religious feeling will be the unforced flowers of life." All of our children deserve this balance!

The invasion of mediocrity in our lives and in our classrooms produces and incalculable loss; the tyranny of modern thought sets limits on mental powers and obscures potential excellence. Good literature can lure it to the surface.

The suggested titles that follow are recent additions to the many fine books available to stimulate creative and critical thought. While all of the books are meant to be shared and discussed, the first eight titles are included as examples of beginning readers that the first grader can handle alone. Note that these titles are more than a few dull words. They do stimulate critical thinking through presenting problems within the child's realm of understanding. They conclude with unique solutions.

References

Dewey, John. *How We Think.* Houghton Mifflin, 1933.
Torrance, E. Paul. *Guiding Creative Talent.* Prentice-Hall, 1962.

Suggested Children's Reading

Easy Readers

Brandenberg, Franz. *Leo and Emily's Zoo.* Illus. by Yossi Abolafia. Greenwillow, 1988. (Ages 4–7).

It was opening day at the zoo. But as Leo and Emily discovered, it is not easy to be a zookeeper. The frogs were at the bottom of the pond. The rabbits had tunneled underground. And there were no lions or giraffes or zebras or monkeys. The zoo visitors were disappointed — until suddenly there was a loud roar. . . .

Coerr, Eleanor. *Chang's Paper Pony.* Illus. by Deborah Kogan Ray. Harper and Row, 1988. (Ages 4–7).

It's the time of the gold rush, and Chang and his grandfather have just come to California from China. They work together in the kitchen of a mining camp.

Chang is very lonely. He wants a pony more than anything else. But the only pony he and Grandpa Li can afford is the painting of a pony that hangs over the kitchen stove. Maybe his friend Big Pete can show him how to pan for gold. Maybe then he can make enough money to buy a pony.

Eleanor Goerr's touching story about loneliness in a new land is warmly captured in Deborah Kogan Ray's pictures.

Degen, Bruce. *The Little Witch and the Riddle.* Illus. by author. Harper and Row, 1980. (Ages 4–7).

Lily is a little witch. She knows just a little magic. So when Grandmother Witch sends her a book of magic spells, Lily can hardly wait to learn more. But the book has a big lock on it, and it won't open until Lily solves a very confusing riddle. Only her friend Otto Ogre can help her find the surprising answer.

Harshman, Terry Webb. *Porcupine's Pajama Party.* Illus. by Doug Cushman. Harper and Row, 1988. (Ages 4–7).

There is a pajama party at Porcupine's house. Otter and Owl are spending the night. Otter wants to try a new cookie recipe. Owl wants to watch Monster Bat on television.

The cookie recipe doesn't work quite the way Otter expected, and the movie scares even Owl. But bedtime turns out to be the scariest — and the funniest — part of Porcupine's wonderful pajama party.

The charm and warm humor of these three pals is sure to tickle beginning readers.

Hoban, Lillan. *The Case of the Two Masked Robbers.* Illus. by author. Harper and Row, 1986. (Ages 4–7).

Two robbers have stolen Mrs. Turtle's eggs from Meadow Marsh Bank. Arabella Raccoon and her twin brother, Albert, decide they will be the ones to catch the robbers and get back the eggs.

But finding clues is more difficult than the twins thought. The woods are scary, and the raccoons keep being mistaken for the robbers. When they finally put all the clues together, they are in for a big surprise . . . and so are the robbers!

Hoff, Syd. *Mrs. Brice's Rice.* Illus. by author. Harper and Row, 1988. (Ages 4–7).

> Mrs. Brice had twenty-five mice.
> She fed her mice
> the finest cheese.
> She washed and dried them
> behind their ears,
> so they were always clean.

Every morning Mrs. Brice and 24 of her mice exercise together; one very small mouse keeps sleeping. Whenever Mrs. Brice sings and plays the piano, 24 mice dance around her; one very small mouse dances on her hand.

In fact, one very small mouse does everything differently. So when there's trouble, who else but one very small mouse comes to the rescue!

Syd Hoff, the inimitable author of many classic *I Can Read Books,* will once again capture young readers' hearts with this charming new story.

Luttrell, Ida. *Mattie and the Chicken Thief.* Illus. by Thacher Hurd. Dodd Mead, 1988. (Ages 4–7).

Did a thief take Mattie's chickens? Mattie thinks so. The hens are gone. She aims to catch the thief and get her hens back. Otherwise, Mattie and Howler, her dog, and Prowler, her cat, will go hungry. The four hens, Dusty, Rusty, Ruffles and Pearl, each laid an egg a day. Mattie cooked two and traded two for meat and milk.

What a trap Mattie builds! It must have worked, because the hens were soon back in the hen house. Mattie never discovered the part Howler and Prowler played in "capturing" the chicken thief, but perhaps that is just as well.

Moore, Lilian. *I'll Met You at the Cucumbers.* Illus. by Sharon Wooding. Atheneum, 1988. (Ages 4–7).

Every week when the farmer's truck full of vegetables went to the Farmer's Market in the city, Junius Mouse went with it. But Adam Mouse did not.

"Are you afraid?" Junius asked. Adam wondered about that. Was he afraid? It was true that everything Junius said about the city sounded rather alarming. Yet it was in the city that Amanda Mouse lived. And she was not frightening. She and Adam were pen friends. Adam wrote down his thoughts and sent them to her, and she answered in lovely notes Adam enjoyed. So when Amanda wanted Adam to visit the city on her birthday, he felt he had to go. "I'll met you at the cucumbers," Amanda said.

The journey was more, much more, than Adam could have imagined. There were other farms to be seen along the way. There was the great bridge and the huge river that ran beneath it. And finally there was Amanda and the sights of the city and the friends who gathered for the birthday party. In spite of the dangers—and they were there, just as Adam had thought—it was a great day.

But the most amazing thing of all was what Adam found out about himself. The thoughts he had been sending to Amanda were poems. He was a poet. And he had never known it.

Critical Thinking

Ackerman, Karen. *Araminta's Paintbox.* Illus. by Betsy Lewin. Atheneum, 1990. (Ages 4–8).

Araminta's doctor father decides to take his family west to answer the call for a doctor in California. The family must *plan* what to take, the route to follow and prepare for unforeseen hardships and dangers. Araminta's uncle gives her a paintbox which she treasures. The box is left behind when the wagon breaks down. The box travels west as well in a variety of hands. Students might *predict* what would have happened to the paintbox if it had not been found by the Mennonite family or if it had been left on the boat docks rather than being rescued by the Army bride.

Agee, John. *The Incredible Painting of Felix Clousseau.* Illus. by author. Farrar, Straus and Giroux, 1988. (Ages 4–8).

Felix Clousseau, an unknown painter, enters a painting in an exhibition with the paintings of the great and famous. His painting of a duck is so lifelike (it quacks) that he wins and the people all flock to buy his lifelike paintings. However, when his volcano painting erupts, the cannon painting explodes and the waterfall painting floods a house, the buyers have Felix put in jail. All paintings are confiscated except one. This one painting of a watchdog which hangs in the palace saves the day when a thief tries to steal the king's jewels. Here is an excellent title for *evaluation.* Should people embrace the new and different regardless of the consequences? Is progress always positive? Should Clousseau have been jailed for giving people what they wanted?

Alderson, Sue Ann. *Ida and the Wool Smugglers.* Illus. by Ann Blades. McElderry, 1987. (Ages 5–8).

Long ago when tall trees grew where cities now stand, farmers settled the islands that lie off the west coast of Canada. On one of those island farms, young Ida lived with her big brother, John, her little sister, Martha, and their mother and father. One spring morning, when everyone else was busy, Ida's mother asked her to take some fresh-baked bread to their neighbors, the Springmans. The Springmans' new baby had just arrived and they would be much too busy for baking.

John, Ida's brother, thought she was too young to go alone. She wasn't even big enough yet to help with the spring sheep run, an annual event at which the sheep were driven into a corral to be shorn. And there was the danger of smugglers who came from the mainland to steal sheep — Ida might encounter them. Mother was sure, however, that Ida would be safe as long as she stayed on the trail. But when Ida — stopping along the way to visit her pet ewe, Tandy, and Tandy's twin lambs — hears a whistle and another in answer, she knows it is the smugglers. She must save Tandy and the twins from them — but how?

This lovingly told story of brave Ida conveys the special feeling of community that existed in pioneer times. Ann Blades's evocative full-color paintings are a perfect complement to the heartwarming tale, in a book to be read and savored time and again.

Allen, Pamela. *The Hidden Treasure.* Illus. by author. Putnam, 1987. (Ages 5–8).

Two brothers argue over a treasure until one is pushed out of a boat and left to drown. The brother who keeps the treasure spends his entire life worrying about it and trying to guard it. The other brother who has no treasure marries and has a happy productive life. *Evaluate . . .* what makes for happiness?

Amoss, Berthe. *Torn in the Middle.* Illus. by the author. Harper and Row, 1988. (Ages 4–7).

Tom's little brother, John, follows him everywhere. Sometimes he gets to be a pest. His big brother, Mark, can do almost anything, but sometimes he yells at Tom. One day Tom-in-the-middle decides he has had enough, puts on his policeman suit and goes away.

Berthe Amoss has lovingly reillustrated in full color her timeless story about the pleasures and dilemmas of being the middle child.

Carlson, Natalie Savage. *Spooky and the Bad Luck Raven.* Illus. by Andrew Glass. Lothrop, 1988. (Ages 5–8).

Crawk! Crawk! Spooky knew the raven meant bad luck the minute he saw the big black bird. Could the witch have sent it to let him know that she had Snowball, the Bascombs' other housecat, back in her clutches?

Bump! Crash! Crack! Broomsticks break and black hats bounce as Spooky springs into action to rescue Snowball. The clever, courageous cat's fourth hair-raising romp is certain to entertain young readers—and make them feel lucky to know a hero like him.

Cole, Johanna. *Dr. Change.* Illus. by Donald Carrick. William Morrow, 1986. (Ages 5–8).

Dr. Change hires a young assistant who supposedly cannot read. The boy discovers that Dr. Change has a book of magic spells which he used to transform himself into a variety of animate and inanimate objects. In trying to escape, Tom has great difficulty but finally manages, with the help of a young girl who uses her wits, to foil the doctor's plans. This is a great book for *forecasting.* What will happen if Tom does not escape? What would happen if Dr. Change's book of spells disappears?

Huck, Charlotte. *Princess Furball.* Illus. by Anita Lobel. Greenwillow, 1989. (Ages 4–8).

In this German version of the Cinderella tale, Princess Furball must achieve her goals through careful *planning.* What strange objects does she take with her on her journey? How will she use them to achieve her goals? How is careful planning sometimes better than depending on luck?

Hughes, Shirley. *Dogger.* Illus. by author. Lothrop, Lee and Shepard, 1987. (Ages 4–7).

Once there was a soft brown dog called Dogger. One of his ears pointed upwards and the other flopped over. His fur was worn in places because he was quite old. Dogger belonged to Dave, who was very fond of him.

This is the endearing story of how Dave's cherished toy was lost and unexpectedly found again. Reassuring and realistic, it captures a familiar experience of childhood and casts a loving light on the family.

Kasza, Keiko. *The Pigs' Picnic.* Illus. by author. Putnam, 1989. (Ages 3–6).

Mr. Pig wants to look his best to take Miss Pig on a picnic. He accepts advice from the lion to borrow his mane, the zebra to borrow his stripes, and from other animals. *Forecast* what will happen when Mr. Pig arrives at Miss Pig's door not looking at all like himself.

Kroll, Steven. *Looking for Daniela: A Romantic Adventure.* Illus. by Anita Lobel. Holiday House, 1988. (Ages 5–8).

Antonio is a performer. He juggles apples and oranges at the piazza. He stretches a tightrope between two trees and walks across it. He does flips in the air and plays his guitar.

Daniela is the daughter of a rich merchant. Each morning, she waves to Antonio from her window. Sometimes, she slips away and dances with him in the piazza.

One day, Antonio discovers that Daniela is missing. She has been kidnapped by bandits. Desperate to rescue her, Antonio sets out with his dog Bruno on an adventurous journey.

LeGuin, Ursula. *Fire and Stone.* Illus. by Laura Marshall. Atheneum, 1989. (Ages 4– 8).

A terrible dragon threatens the village. Since the people are never sure when the dragon will appear, they man a warning tower and ring bells when he is sighted. Then all the people run to Rocky Pond and hide in the water until the dragon leaves. This, of course, is both frightening and disruptive to village life. How can this problem be solved? What can they do to rid the village of this danger? Once students have come up with a solution they will be surprised at the easy solution found by Min and Podo, two children in the story.

McDonald, Megan. *Is This a House for Hermit Crab?* Illus. by author. Orchard, 1990. (Ages 3–6).

Here is a perfect story hour book to introduce predicting or forecasting. Hermit Crab, who needs a home safe from the pricklepine fish, goes wandering about trying out a variety of shelters. After he tries the bucket, the fishing net, the rock and other places, the reader is asked, "Is this a house for hermit crab?" Children can predict whether or not the proposed shelter will work and why or why not.

McKissack, Patricia. *Flossie and the Fox.* Illus. by Rachel Isadora. Dial, 1987. (Ages 4–8).

Flossie lies in the Piney Woods and is told by Big Mama to take a basket of eggs to Miss Viola who lives on the other side of the woods. Big Mama warns FLossie to watch out for the fox since "that critter sure do love eggs." In the woods, the first creature Flossie meets is the fox. How will she get to Miss Viola's with the eggs? Here is a problem to ponder and young readers will be surprised at Flossie's solution.

Manes, Steven. *Life Is No Fair.* Illus. by author. Coward, 1986. (Ages 4–8).

Here is a series of short problems with the problem presented on one page and the solution the next. "Willard Twombly worried that when his family moved away from the old neighborhood that he would never make another friend." Faced with this problem, students often suggest that he take a friend with him; that a friend will live next door to the new house; that a playground full of friends will be across the street; that he finds a pet for a friend or that he has an imaginary friend. No matter how many guesses students make they almost never guess the imaginative solution Steven Manes has for this and other problems in the book.

Martin, Jacqueline Briggs. *Bizzy Bones and the Lost Quilt.* Illus. by Stella Ormai. Lothrop, 1988. (Ages 3–6).

Bizzy Bones's quilt is special. It goes everywhere with him and gives him good dreams every night – until it disappears.

Uncle Ezra does his best to console Bizzy, but the heartbroken little mouse knows that nothing can take the place of the lost quilt.

Every young child who has experienced the loss of a treasure will understand how Bizzy feels, and will rejoice with him as three new friends, expert finders and fixers, help bring the third Bizzy Bones story to its joyful conclusion.

Moore, Inga. *The Sorcerer's Apprentice.* Illus. by author. Macmillan, 1989. (Ages 4–8).

In this beautifully illustrated retelling of an old tale, Inga Moore tells of the adventuresome young boy who applies for a job as a sorcerer's apprentice. The boy is fascinated by the sorcerer's many spells and at the same time does not like the work he has to do . . . particularly carrying buckets of water up many flights of stairs to fill the cauldron each day. When the sorcerer leaves for the day, the boy casts a spell on the broom and orders it to carry water. The broom obeys but the spell cannot be turned off and the sorcerer's workshop is flooded. Forecast what will happen when the sorcerer returns.

Nordquist, Sven. *The Hat Hunt.* Illus. by author. R and S Books, 1988. (Ages 5–8).

Grandpa has a hat which he never takes off, except when he goes to bed. But one day it's gone! Still in his nightshirt, Grandpa pursues it all over town, to Mrs. Hen's, the mysterious Someone's house, and Tailor Button-Up's shop. And still it eludes him. Instead, Grandpa keeps finding things that seem strangely familiar: a tin soldier, a watch chain, a penknife, a magnet and a whistle. But it is not until he is catapulted off a motorcycle into a nice summery meadow that Grandpa remembers the childhood in which all these small objects played a part.

Polette, Keith. *The Winter Duckling.* Illus. by Clovis Martin. Milliken, 1990. (Ages 3–6).

A small wood duck decides not to fly south for the winter. He wants to see snow. When his flock leaves he watches the other birds prepare for winter while he plays. He even watches the old woman across the pond gather berries and nuts and firewood for the winter to come. When the snows arrive there is no room in the other birds' nests for the wood duck. He falls in the snow and is rescued by the old woman and taken to her cottage. She offers him the option of flying south "while he still can" or staying with her. However she is preparing a big cooking pot while she is talking to him. Decide what the duckling should do.

Pryor, Bonnie. *The Porcupine Mouse.* Illus. by Maryjane Begin. Morrow, 1988. (Ages 4–7).

Louie and Dan were two little mice. They were brothers and best friends. One day they left their home to find a place of their own . . . but not before Mama Mouse gave them some very good advice: "Always eat a good breakfast. Keep a clean handkerchief in your pocket. And never forget that the world is full of cats and owls."

Louis, a timid mouse, was content to set up housekeeping in a cozy little cottage. But it didn't take long for Dan to forget every word that Mama Mouse had said.

Schertle, Alice. *Gus Wanders Off.* Illus. by Cheryl Harness. Lothrop, 1988. (Ages 4–7).

Mama told Gus not to wander off, and Gus doesn't mean to. But when his teacher's dog, Hannibal, comes by, Gus can't help following that wag-a-lag tail down the street. Soon the streets become unfamiliar, and Gus doesn't know which way to go. With the help of his teacher, Mrs. Bundy, Gus figures out how to retrace his steps, from the fish store to the playground to the park on the corner, all the way home.

This entertaining, reassuring story is perfect for an adult and a young child to read together and talk about. Children will enjoy spotting the clues that lead Gus back to Mama, picking up some basics of neighborhood navigation—including the importance of knowing your address—on the way.

Steig, William. *Brave Irene.* Illus. by author. Farrar, Straus and Giroux, 1986. (Ages 4–7).

Brave Irene is Irene Bobbin, the dressmaker's daughter. Her mother, Mrs. Bobbin, isn't feeling so well and can't possibly deliver the beautiful ball gown she's made for the duchess to wear that evening. So plucky Irene volunteers to get the gown to the palace on time, in spite of the fierce snowstorm that's brewing—quite an errand for a little girl.

But where there's a will, there's a way, as Irene proves in the danger-fraught adventure that follows. She must defy the wiles of the wicked wind, her most formidable opponent, and overcome many obstacles before she completes her mission. Surely, this winning heroine will inspire every child to cheer her on.

Thiele, Colin. *Farmer Schulz's Ducks.* Illus. by Mary Milton. Harper and Row, 1988. (Ages 5–8).

Farmer Schulz loves his ducks. Every day they go for a swim in the nearby Onkaparinga River. The only trouble is that they have to cross a busy road to get there and back again. How can they do this in safety? Farmer Schulz asks his children Gretchen, Adolf and Helga for ideas, but it is little Anna who finally solves the problem.

Farmer Schulz's Ducks is a beautifully written story, full of warmth and humor.

Wood, Don, and Wood, Audrey. *Heckedy Peg.* Illus. by Don Wood. Harcourt Brace, 1987. (Ages 4–8).

A mother leaves her seven children one day promising to bring each a gift if they will not open the door to strangers or play with fire. Heckedy Peg, the witch, persuades the children to let her in and quickly changes them all to food. She then loads her cart and takes them to her cottage in the woods. When the mother comes home and finds her children missing she is determined to find them. A small bird leads her to the witch's hut where she demands entrance. "I want my children back!" she shouts. Heckedy Peg gives the mother one chance to save her children. She must guess which child has been turned into which food. By knowing what gift each child asked for and associating that with the various foods, the mother is able to save her children. Can the reader solve the problem before reading the solution in the story?

Yorinks, Arthur. *Oh, Brother.* Illus. by Richard Egileski. Farrar, Straus and Giroux, 1989. (Ages 4–8).

Two brothers who do not get along with each other are rescued from a shipwreck and find themselves alone in New York City. They escape from "Rotten's Home for Lost Boys" and turn to crime as pickpockets. One day they choose the wrong victim and get tangled in an old man's suspenders. The old man takes the boys home and teaches them his trade, tailoring. When the old man dies the boys have to find a way to keep the business going without having customers discover that they are dealing with children. Predict what they will do.

8

Expanding the Horizons of Young Thinkers

Informational books are rare treasures. The best are written with knowlege and enthusiasm and are beautifully and accurately illustrated. Non-fiction books today are a far cry from those of 10 or 20 years ago. With improvement in color art technology and with the goal of authors to be entertaining as well as factual, today's books are a treat for the eye and mind alike. The best of the informational books for children attempt to answer questions *and* to stimulate the reader to ask new questions. It is through literature that the child can wonder and confirm or deny those wonderings.

In books for very young children it is sometimes difficult to distinguish fiction from non-fiction. In Colin Eisler's *Cats Know Best* (Dial Books for Young Readers, 1988), the child will see many cats performing their daily activities in exquisitely realistic pictures. Yet notice the delicacy and grace of the text: "Where is the best place to be on a wintry evening? Cats know — in front of a warm fireplace! And where's the best place for keeping cool on a hot summer day? Stretched out on a branch in the leafy shade of an apple tree. Where is the milk the freshest, the mice the most plump? Cats know, just as they know best how to groom themselves, take care of their kittens and have a splendid mock battle with each other." Obviously this book was well researched by both author and artist. Enough facts emerge about cats from the simple text and illustrations to satisfy that upper left brain quadrant need for facts. The questions asked will stimulate the child to think about what he or she is hearing and seeing as well as use any previous knowledge the child possesses about cats to predict what will be on the next page (a lower left quadrant thinking skill).

Non-fiction books are available at almost every interest level for children. The same topic can be explored in simple picture book form or in a more comprehensive narrative text. There are few topics that are not covered and it would be impossible here to touch upon even a representative sample of titles available in this text. Instead, we have provided a representative group of books and activities that can form the base for sharing a variety of informational books with children.

The Natural World

In a country that is rapidly destroying its natural beauty and resources, what better books to share with children than those that develop an appreciation for nature and the environment.

A book that makes an emotional impact on the young environmentalist is Ruth Brown's *The World That Jack Built* (Dutton, 1991). Through sparce text and beautiful illustrations, Ruth Brown shows an ideal view of nature with clear streams, green meadows and lush forests. She then contrasts this view with showing "another" valley with blackened forests, polluted streams and bare meadows. A final illustration shows polluted waste coming from a factory. Few words are needed.

An old title which is as relevant today as when it was published is *The Big Snow* by Berta and Elmer Hader.

As wild geese were flying across the sky Mrs. Cottontail told littlest rabbit that the cold winter days were near. When fat groundhog saw the geese flying overhead he knew it was nearly time for his winter nap. The animals of the field and wood knew it was time to prepare for winter. They were right, and were helped through the long, cold days by a little old man and woman who put food out for them until spring came.

What can children do today to help wild creatures survive the winter?

In informational books for the very youngest the information is often conveyed through the pictures rather than the text. In Ruth Krauss's *Big and Little* (Scholastic, 1988) the child will discover:

> big forests love little trees
> big fields love little flowers
> big monkeys love little monkeyshines
> and I love you

So begins this simple, evocative and delightfully impish poem about big things and little things and a child's special place in a loving world. The color illustrations by Mary Szilagyi depict a spunky little boy's explorations of this world, as the landscape shifts from country to city, and the seasons change from spring to summer, fall and winter. The little boy's understanding of love changes, too, as his relationship with his pet cat grows and takes on greater meaning at the surprise conclusion of this beautiful book.

Informational books abound on every aspect of the natural world. Trevor Smith's *Amazing Lizards* (Knopf, 1990) has brilliant photographs

accompanied by an exciting text. Readers will be amazed at the information
provided in Alexandra Parson's *Amazing Cats* (Knopf, 1990). Simple ex-
periments to involve young readers are included in Patricia Lauber's *How
We Learned the Earth Is Round*, (Harper-Collins, 1990) and Seymour Simon
can always be depended upon to provide an understandable account of any
science subject as he does with *Oceans* (Morrow, 1990), made understandable by simple charts and graphs as well as stunning photographs.

No discussion of non-fiction would be complete without mentioning
the "Magic School Bus" series written by Joanna Cole and illustrated by
Bruce Degan. Children can spend hours with these books. The newest, *The
Magic School Bus Lost in the Solar System* takes teacher Mrs. Frizzle and
her class to outer space. The clever illustrations, accurate information and
humor make every book in this series a winner.

New information for young children must be presented first in simple-to-understand terms and in a familiar context or setting. The best of informational books, then, must follow this pattern. Tomie de Paola is a master writer/illustrator of both fiction and non-fiction books for young children. He thoroughly understands the need to begin at the child's level of understanding before presenting new information. A brief description of his *Quicksand Book* (Holiday House, 1977) illustrates this.

> Poor Jungle Girl!   (What child hasn't taken a fall!)
> She falls into the quicksand.   (What child hasn't gotten all messy!)
> Jungle boys finds her.   (What child doesn't want to be rescued?)
> Jungle Girl starts to sink while Jungle Boy tells her:
>
> > where and how quicksand forms
> > why people sink in quicksand
> > what happens to animals in quicksand
> > how peole can watch out for quicksand
> > what people should do if they fall into quicksand

By understanding Jungle Girl's plight as she sinks lower and lower into the quicksand, the child *wants to know* more about quicksand (and the ultimate fate of Jungle Girl). But Jungle Girl does not sink forever and the tale ends happily and with a hands-on quicksand experiment for the child to try.

Exploring the Past

Young children have no sense of history since they have not lived long enough to experience a history of their own. Many bright children avoid books about other lands, other times or people different from themselves simply because they have no prior knowledge or "hooks" to hang this new information on. Non-fiction books can turn vague imaginings to knowledge and truth. Much, for example, can be learned from only the illustrations in *St. George and the Dragon* by Margaret Hodges. You and your child can take an armchair journey to the Middle Ages with this beautiful book.

ACTIVITY: Look at the picture on the right: The Red Cross Knight and Princess Una are on a journey to fight a terrible dragon. Study the picture of the Red Cross Knight. Study his armor which he wears to protect him on his great adventure. The Princess Una's cloak provides no protection. Design a dress for Una to wear to protect her in the way armor protects the knight. Use a different piece of paper to design and drawn an anti-dragon dress for Una. Show how your new design is better and more useful for a princess who helps fight dragons.

Books which are carefully researched to present times in history, places in the world or peoples of many cultures can be invaluable in building the child's base of understanding. In another Middle Ages picture book tale, Donald Carrick tells of Harald who has always wanted to be one of the Baron's knights. Their bright, clanking armor and brave exploits entrance him. But one spring, the knights, without so much as a by-your-leave, take over the land farmed by Harald's family. They trample the crops and eat the livestock. There seems to be no way to get rid of the invaders, until Harald comes up with an idea. Will it work? He and his parents can't be sure, but they plunge into the creation of the biggest and most terrifying knight that anyone has ever seen . . . and made entirely of straw! In *Harald and the Giant Knight* (Clarion, 1982) children will visit another time and another place. The journey, however, begins with the familiar, a family with a problem, someone taking something that belongs to you . . . and the familiar problem is solved against the lavish and accurately illustrated background of the Middle Ages.

Picture books which tell a story in which the young child becomes involved, can also accurately and often lovingly depict a variety of cultures.

Books by Paul Gobel, carefully researched for authenticity of background, tell tales of the early American Indian. In his *Girl Who Loved Wild Horses,* young children will empathize with the Indian heroine who is torn between her love for family and for the beautiful wild horses that call to her. The illustrations depict the art and the culture of the Plains Indians.

The tribe moved from place to place and kept horses to carry their belongings and to hunt buffalo. The girl loved the horses and understood them in a special way. During the storm she was carried away by the horses to a strange land where she and the horses were welcomed by a wild stallion. A year later, when hunters from the girl's tribe found her and took her home, she longed to return to her first love, the horses.

Television provides a few role models for the children of today to emulate. Certainly the child's most important role model is the parent, but how fortunate is the child who meets at an early age those who have achieved greatness in history. There are countless fine books available to introduce great lives to young children that begin with the child's level of understanding. In *Me and Willie and Pa* (Simon and Schuster, 1973), by F.N. Monjo, the story is told by Tad. Tad's father, Abraham Lincoln, emerges as a real, caring parent as he takes Tad into his bed recognizing Tad's terrible feeling of being left alone after the death of his brother Willie. *The Glorious Flight* (Viking, 1983) by Alice and Martin Provensen tells the story of Louis Bleriot, one of the truly great pioneers of aviation. His five children watch him build 11 different flying machines before he made his first successful flight over the English Channel, flying from France to England in 37 minutes. Rather than including a lengthy description of each of the 11 models, the authors show marvelous illustrations of each so that the child can visually follow the development of the flying machine.

The choices are nearly endless. Whatever book the parent chooses to share that is sourced in the real world, he or she is providing an experience that is enhanced by all of the books shared previously. We could liken the consciousness of each child to a giant jigsaw puzzle, with pieces missing here and there. Each literary experience can perhaps fit a missing piece of the puzzle into the whole, until a worldview is achieved which is solid and beautiful.

The newer titles suggested at the end of this chapter are by no means meant to be first choices in sharing informational books with your child. The field is vast and the titles included here are meant to be representative of the vast treasure storehouse awaiting you and your child in the library.

In summary, the guidelines for use in sharing fine literature with children are not difficult to follow. Always begin with the child's world and his or her level of understanding. Remember that the patterns of written language are impressed on the brain through hearing a wonderful book read aloud. Children later use these patterns in their own thinking, speaking and ultimately reading and writing. Forced reading instruction before the child has sufficiently matured neurological systems can cause damage later on. Helping children to see patterns and relationships in words and ideas is the key to full development of each of the brain's four quadrants. Finally, in the words of Bill Martin, Jr., "The goal of language instruction is not to develop skills in and of themselves, but to help the child claim his or her humanity through the use of language."

Suggested Children's Reading

For the Very Youngest

Rockwell, Anne. *Things to Play With*. Illus. by author. Dutton, 1988. (Ages 2–4).
  Music boxes and mailing tubes. Dolls and dandelions. Wagons and wading pools. Swings, soap bubbles and skateboards. This big and colorful book is bursting with objects that children love to play with. Inside and out, at school or a party, at the beach or on snow and ice, the animal youngsters in this book have fun with all kinds of things. Young readers will delight in learning and recognizing fascinating and familiar playthings, grouped or patterned in special ways.

_____. *Trains*. Illus. by author. Dutton, 1988. (Ages 2–4).
  Freight trains. Passenger trains. Monorails. Subways. Different trains go all kinds of places — over city streets, through the countryside, even underground. A colorful book that will delight and add knowledge for every child who loves things that go. All aboard!

Counting

Giganti, Paul, Jr. *How Many Snails, a Counting Book*. Illus. by Donald Crews. Greenwillow, 1988. (Ages 2–4).
  You and your child will need to look very carefully at the pictures. This is not just another counting book. You must look for specific details: spots on the dogs, stripes on the snails, icing on the cupcakes. There are many things to look for and count, and many hours of fun and satisfaction, for the counter.

Animals

Arnosky, Jim. *Come Out, Muskrats*. Illus. by author. Lothrop, Lee and Shepard, 1989. (Ages 3–6).
  Full-color paintings and sparce, poetic text evoke the twilight world of muskrats who swim "through the setting sun" to start their night's frolic. The day-into-night setting and the quiet conclusion make this book an ideal bedtime read-aloud. Muskrats are portrayed accurately in their habitat through the artist's skill, meticulous observation and deep respect for the natural world.

Brown, Ruth. *Ladybug, Ladybug*. Illus. by author. E.P. Dutton, 1988. (Ages 2–4).

Blown off the palm of a young boy's hand and then caught by the breeze, Lady-bug begins her long flight home. In an extended version of the well-loved nursery rhyme, she flies over the wheat field, past the pond, through the leafy wood, finally reaching her nest where her children lie safely asleep. The lovely illustrations evoke the languor and beauty of a summer day in the country.

Burton, Marilee Robin. *Tail Toes Eyes Ears Nose.* Illus. by author. Harper and Row, 1988. (Ages 2–4).
   Who has a curly tail?! Whose ears are hidden? Turn the page and find out! Here is a delightful guessing game that highlights eight familiar animals and then puts them all together for a final surprise. Big shapes and bold colors create a playful book that parent and child will share again and again.

MacQuitty, Miranda (editor). *Side by Side.* Photographs by author. E.P. Putnam, 1988. (Ages 4–8).
   All sorts of animals live close to other kinds of animals. Some are partners and help each other, while others are parasites and harm the animals they live with. *Side by Side* tells about some of these weird and wonderful relationships, with beautiful photographs, from shrimp that clean between the teeth of fish to plants that can be partners with animals.

Ryden, Hope. *Wild Animals of America ABC.* Photographs by author. Lodestar-Dut-ton, 1988. (Ages 4–8).
   Here is a unique ABC of wild animals from the sunning alligator to the regal zone-tailed hawk. In full-color photographs, the child will meet an array of familiar and little-known creatures. Some, like the skunk, can easily be detected near your home; others, like the xanthid crab, lie hidden on the ocean floor. This is a book for browsing and learning and one that will start the child looking for wild animals living nearby.

Simon, Seymour. *Animal Fact, Animal Fable.* Illus. by Diane deGroat. Crown, 1979. (Ages 4–8).
   Here is scientific fact presented as a guessing game. A statement about an animal appears on one page: "Fact or Fable, An owl is a wise bird." The next page gives the answer along with brief, accurate information. The illustrations are fun and the message for the young child is "just because it is in a book, it is not necessarily true!"

Yolen, Jane. *Owl Moon.* Illus. by John Schoenherr. Philomel, 1987. (Ages 4–8).
   With a perfect blend of pictures and text this magical book follows a father and his daughter through snow-covered woods in search of a Great Horned Owl. The words and the illustrations place the reader outside in the cold woodlands and into the warm relationship between a father and his daughter who share a reverence and respect for nature.

Nature

Branley, Franklyn M. *The Sun Is Our Nearest Star.* Illus. by Don Madden. Crowell, 1988. (Ages 5–8).
   This is a true non-fiction book for the young child. The sun has been shining for millions of years. It gives us light and keeps us warm. Without the sun there would be no plants or animals. Without the sun there would be no life on earth. What is the sun? The sun is our daytime star, the star closest to all the earth. In this brightly

illustrated book, young children will discover what the sun is made of, how hot it is and how far away, and how long it takes the light from the sun to reach the earth. A simple experiment is included to show children how the light from the sun makes things grow.

Coucher, Helen. *Rain Forest.* Illus. by author. Farrar, Straus and Giroux, 1988. (Ages 4–8).
    In the rain forest, creatures live peacefully. Sloths, anteaters and tapirs roam its cool floor. Toucans and macaws nest in its canopy. And, high above its exotic foliage, butterflies flutter. Jaguar prowls his lush kingdom. But suddenly a cry of alarm sounds through the rain forest. Something even more powerful than Jaguar is threatening this world, and the creatures know that a major change is coming to their lives. Even the very youngest child will enjoy this oversized, boldy illustrated picture book.

King-Smith, Dick. *Cuckoobush Farm.* Illus. by Kazuko. Greenwillow, 1987. (Ages 3–6).
    It is springtime at Cuckoobush Farm. There are baby birds in their nests, baby rabbits in their burrows and newborn lambs in the field. Hazel, who lives at Cuckoobush Farm, loves them all. As the seasons change and more animals are born — lambs, piglets, calves — Hazel is delighted. And on Christmas Day two new babies arrive at Cuckoobush Farm — babies who will need (and are sure to get) — a big sister's love.

McCloskey, Robert. *Time of Wonder.* Illus. by author. Viking, 1957. A Caldecott Medal Winner. (Ages 3–6).
    Through poetic text and full color illustrations the author shares sights, senses and feelings of summer spent near the ocean on an island off the Maine seacoast. Summer vacation is a time to live and love the world of nature as the weather changes and the tides come and go. The animals, insects and birds show their special characteristics, and the plants change. As children go exploring during this time of wonder, young children will explore as well.

MacDonald, Gordon. *The Little Island.* Illus. by Leonard Weisgard. Doubleday, 1946. A Caldecott Award winner. (Ages 3–6).
    The little island lived alone in the ocean watching the changes the seasons brought to the plants and animals of the island. One day a small kitten came to the island with some people on a picnic. The kitten thought the island was very little and must be very lonely. But the kitten discovered that the island was not separated from the rest of the world at all, but connected to the land under water. The little island was content with its life as a part of the world, yet having a life of its own, surrounded by bright blue sea. A treasure to share again and again!

Tejima. *Woodpecker Forest.* Illus. by author. Philomel, 1989. (Ages 3–6).
    In a faraway forest, a young woodpecker flies for the first time. He clings bravely to a nearby tree until night comes. But when strange sounds echo through the darkness, hollow trees seem to stare and dark shadows sway in the moonlight. Here is the excitement and fear of a first trip out alone that will touch parents and children alike.

Other Times and Places

Gerstein, Mordicai. *The Mountains of Tibet*. Illus. by author. Harper and Row, 1987. (Ages 4–8).
    All of his life a woodcutter longs to travel and see the world. But he grows old without leaving his valley in the mountains of Tibet. When he dies, he's sudddenly offered the chance to live again, in any form and in any place he likes. The universe with its spectacular array of stars and creatures parades past him. His head spins. Shall he join the animal kingdom or become a dancer in another land? Shall he live in a village or on a distant planet? This is a simple journey through the diversity of life with all of its choices.

Handforth, Thomas. *Mei Li*. Illus. by author. Doubleday, 1938. A Caldecott Medal winner. (Ages 5–8).
    Mei Li was busy helping her mother prepare for the visit of the kitchen god who would come on New Year's Eve. She listened sadly to her brother's plans for going to the New Year's fair because little girls always had to stay home. However, Mei Li gathers her pennies and three lucky marbles and tags along with brother to the fair. Arriving home just in time to greet the kitchen god, Mei Li learns that her home is her kingdom. A beautifully illustrated glimpse of life in long ago China.

Real People

Brighton, Catherine. *Five Secrets in a Box*. Illus. by author. E.P. Dutton, 1987. (Ages 5–8).
    The box is a fine wrought gold, and it sits on a table crowded with strange and fascinating objects — Galileo's instruments. His small daughter Virginia opens the box and finds five objects that reveal the world to her and other children in new and wonderful ways. In richly textured paintings, the author/artist creates a glowing Renaissance world. Her unique view of it through a child's eyes gives children everywhere a fascinating and memorable insight into the magic of science and the working of one of the world's greatest minds.

d'Aulaire, Ingri and Edgar. *Abraham Lincoln*. Illus. by Edgar d'Aulaire. Doubleday, 1939. A Caldecott Medal winner. (Ages 5–8).
    Here is a simple introduction to the life of Abraham Lincoln from birth in a Kentucky log cabin to the presidency. Included in the retelling of this humble gifted man's life are many popular, humorous anecdotes. The pictures reveal authentic settings of the time.

Gerrard, Roy. *Sir Frances Drake: His Daring Deeds*. Illus. by author. Farrar, Straus and Giroux, 1988. (Ages 5–8).
> When Francis Drake was only ten,
> he went to sea with grown-up men,
> And flabbergasted all the crew
> by quickly learning what to do.

    Imagine being the captain of your own ship, exploring new lands, battling Spaniards on the high seas, even drinking tea with the Queen of England. Sir Francis Drake did all this, and now 400 years after he defeated the Spanish Armada, you can join him. Unusual, authentic illustrations and lilting verse do bring another time and place alive for children.

U.S. History

Abisch, Roz. *The Pumpkin Heads*. Illus. by author. Prentice-Hall, 1968. (Ages 4–8).

————. *Sweet Betsy from Pike*. Illus. by author. McCalls, 1970. (Ages 4–8).

Aliki. *The Many Lives of Benjamin Franklin*. Illus. by author. Prentice-Hall, 1977. (Ages 4–8).

————. *The Story of Johnny Appleseed*. Illus. by author. Prentice-Hall, 1963. (Ages 4–8).

————. *A Weed Is a Flower*. Illus. by author. Prentice-Hall, 1965. (Ages 4–8).

Baker, Betty. *The Pig War*. Illus. by Robert Lopshire. Harper, 1969. (Ages 4–8).

Bangs, Edward. *Yankee Doodle*. Illus. by author. Parents, 1976. (Ages 3–6).

Benchley, Nathaniel. *George the Drummer Boy*. Illus. by Don Bolognese. Harper, 1977. (Ages 3–6).

————. *Sam the Minute Man*. Illus. by Arnold Lobel. Harper, 1969. (Ages 3–6).

————. *Small Wolf*. Illus. by Joan Sandin. Harper, 1972. (Ages 3–6).

Bethell, Jean. *Three Cheers for Mother Jones!* Illus. by author. Holt, 1980. (Ages 4–8).

Brandt, Betty. *Special Delivery*. Illus. by Kathy Haubrich. Carolrhoda, 1988. (Ages 4–8).

Brenner, Barbara. *Wagon Wheels*. Illus. by Don Bolognese. Harper, 1978. (Ages 5–8).

Bulla, Clyde Robert. *Washington's Birthday*. Illus. by Don Bolognese. Crowell, 1967. (Ages 4–8).

Dalgliesh, Alice. *The Thanksgiving Story*. Illus. by Helen Sewell. Scribner, 1954. (Ages 4–8).

d' Aulaire, Ingri Mortenson. *Abraham Lincoln*. Illus. by author. Doubleday, 1939, 1957. (Ages 4–8).

————. *Pocahontas*. Illus. by author. Doubleday, 1946. (Ages 4–8).

de Paola, Tomie. *An Early American Christmas*. Illus. by author. Holiday, 1987. (Ages 3–6).

Dewey, Ariane. *Laffite, the Pirate*. Illus. by author. Greenwillow, 1985. (Ages 4–8).

Haley, Gail E. *Jack Jouett's Ride*. Illus. by author. Viking, 1973. (Ages 5–8).

Harvey, Brett. *Cassie's Journey*. Illus. by Deborah Ray. Holiday, 1988. (Ages 6–9).

————. *Immigrant Girl*. Illus. by Deborah Ray. Holiday, 1987. (Ages 6–9).

————. *My Prairie Year*. Illus. by Deborah Ray. Holiday, 1986. (Ages 6–9).

Haskins, Jim. *The Statue of Liberty*. Illus. by author. Lerner, 1986. (Ages 6–9).

Hiser, Berniece T. *The Adventure of Charlie and His Wheat-Straw Hat.* Illus. by Marcy Szilagyi. Dodd, 1986. (Ages 6–9).

Jones, Rebecca C. *The Biggest (and Best) Flag That Ever Flew.* Illus. by author. Cornell Maritime, 1988. (Ages 6–9).

Kellogg, Steven. *Johnny Appleseed.* Illus. by author. Morrow, 1988. (Ages 4–8).

_____. *Pecos Bill.* Illus. by author. Morrow, 1986. (Ages 4–8).

Key, Francis Scott. *The Star-Spangled Banner.* Illus. by Peter Spier. Doubleday, 1973. (Ages 6–9).

Lawson, Robert. *They Were Strong and Good.* Illus. by author. Viking, 1940. (Ages 6–9).

Levinson, Riki. *Watch the Stars Come Out.* Illus. by Diane Goode. Dutton, 1985. (Ages 4–8).

Lobel, Arnold. *On the Day Peter Stuyvesant Sailed into Town.* Illus. by author. Harper, 1971. (Ages 4–8).

Longfellow, Henry Wadsworth. *Paul Revere's Ride.* Illus. by Nancy Winslow Parker. Greenwillow, 1985. (Ages 4–8).

Maestro, Betsy. *The Story of the Statue of Liberty.* Illus. by Giulio Maestro. Lothrop, 1986. (Ages 6–9).

Monjo, F.N. *The Drinking Gourd.* Illus. by Fred Brenner. Harper, 1970. (Ages 4–8).

_____. *Indian Summer.* Illus. by Anita Lobel. Harper, 1968. (Ages 4–8).

_____. *The One Bad Thing About Father.* Illus. by Anita Lobel. Harper, 1970. (Ages 4–8).

Nixon, Joan Lowery. *Beats Me Claude.* Illus. by Tracey C. Pearson. Viking, 1986. (Ages 4–8).

_____. *Fat Chance, Claude.* Illus. by Tracey C. Pearson. Viking, 1987. (Ages 4–8).

_____. *If You Say So, Claude.* Illus. by Lorinda Cauley. Warne, 1980. (Ages 4–8).

Petersham, Maud. *An American ABC.* Illus. by author. Macmillan, 1941. (Ages 4–8).

Precek, Katharine Wilson. *Penny in the Road.* Illus. by Patricia Cullen-Clark. Macmillan, 1989. (Ages 5–8).

Rappaport, Doreen. *The Boston Coffee Party.* Illus. by Emily Arnold McCully. Harper, 1988. (Ages 6–10).

_____. *Trouble at the Mines.* Illus. by Joan Sandin. Crowell, 1987. (Ages 6–9).

Showers, Paul. *Columbus Day.* Illus. by Ed Emberley. Crowell, 1965. (Ages 6–8).

Spier, Peter. *The Erie Canal.* Illus. by author. Doubleday, 1970. (Ages 4–8).

_____. *The Legend of New Amsterdam.* Illus. by author. Doubleday, 1979. (Ages 4–8).

_____. *Star Spangled Banner.* Illus. by author. Doubleday, 1973. (Ages 5–9).

Turkle, Brinton. *The Adventures of Obadiah.* Illus. by author. Viking, 1977. (Ages 5–8).

_____. *Obadiah the Bold.* Illus. by author. Viking, 1965. (Ages 5–8).

_____. *Thy Friend, Obadiah.* Illus. by author. Viking, 1969. (Ages 5–8).

Turner, Ann. *Dakota Dugout.* Illus. by Ronald Himler. Macmillan, 1985. (Ages 5–8).

_____. *Heron Street.* Illus. by Lisa Desimni. Harper, 1989. (Ages 4–8).

Waber, Bernard. *Just Like Abraham Lincoln.* Illus. by author. Houghton, 1964. (Ages 4–8).

Winter, Jeanette. *Follow the Drinking Gourd.* Illus. by author. Knopf, 1988. (Ages 5–9).

9

A Booklist for Productive Thinking

Sample Books and Activities

Ahlberg, Janet. *The Jolly Postman or Other People's Letters*. Illus. by Allan Ahlberg. Little, Brown, 1986. (Ages 3–6).

In this zany collection of letters from famous fairy tale characters, Goldilocks apologizes to the three bears, Hobgoblin Supplies, Ltd. sends a flyer to the Wicked Witch and Cinderella receives a book offer among other interesting correspondence. In this flexible thinking approach to fairy tale land, students can write their own letters from one famous character to another.

Allard, Harry. *Miss Nelson Has a Field Day*. Illus. by James Marshall. Houghton Mifflin, 1985. (Ages 4–8).

Flexible thinking abounds from the names of the characters (Principal Blandsworth, Coach Armstrong) to the interesting situation. The losing football team receives a new coach, the terrible Coach Swamp, who is determined to change things. Here is a catalyst for great "what if" stories to look at stereotypes. What if a boy were in charge of the girl's cheerleading team? What if the principal taught first grade for a day? What if the teachers became students and the students became the teachers for a day?

Bang, Molly. *The Paper Crane*. Illus. by author. Greenwillow, 1985. (Ages 4–8).

Here is an original idea beautifully illustrated. A mysterious man enters a restaurant and pays for his dinner with a paper crane that magically comes alive and dances. What original stories could students create by bringing to life an inanimate object?

Bond, Michael. *More About Paddington*. Illus. by Peggy Fortnum. Houghton Mifflin, 1962. (Ages 6–10).

One of the many adventures of this lovable bear describes the day he decided to wallpaper his room. When he was finished, he discovered that he could not get out because he had papered over the door and windows (*fluency*). How many ways can you think of for Paddington to find the door and windows?

Bunting, Eve. *Scary, Scary Halloween*. Illus. by Jan Brett. Clarion, 1986. (Ages 4–8).

A story of trick-or-treaters and a mysterious sheeted creature that pursues them. How can you *elaborate* on a basic Halloween costume (ghost, witch, etc.) to make it more interesting?

Carrick, Carol. *What Happened to Patrick's Dinosaurs?* Illus. by Donald Carrick. Clarion, 1986. (Ages 4–8).

We know dinosaurs no longer roam the earth. There are theories why they do not exist but Patrick comes up with a most *original* explanation for their disappearance. What explanations can the reader give *before* reading the story?

Cazet, Denys. *December 24th.* Illus. by author. Bradbury, 1986. (Ages 4–8).

When his grandchildren come to his home to celebrate his December 24th birthday, Grandpa Rabbit pretends ignorance of the occasion by appearing in costumes suitable to other holidays. Think *flexibly*. What problems might arise if we celebrated Halloween on Valentine's Day or celebrated Christmas at Easter?

Christelow, Eileen. *The Robbery at the Diamond Dog Diner.* Illus. by author. Clarion, 1986. (Ages 4–8).

After hiding her friend Lola's diamonds inside newly delivered eggs to protect them from thieves, the thieves kidnap Glenda Feathers, convinced she has laid diamond-filled eggs. Think of an *original* way for her to escape.

Cole, Babette. *King Change-a-lot.* Illus. by author. Putnam, 1988. (Ages 4–8).

Prince Change-a-lot thinks his parents are a royal pain in the diaper. They've allowed the kingdom to be overrun by rampaging dragons, beastly blubber worms, and bad fairies cooking up rotten spells. Taking matters into his own hands, the prince rubs his potty and summons a baby genie who not only sees eye to eye with his young highness, but is prepared to lend a hand with some "improvements" (*flexible thinking*).

He tried the same trick on his own potty and out came a baby genie who could understand baby language!

_____. *Prince Cinders*. Illus. by author. Putnam, 1989. (Ages 4–8).
Poor Prince Cinders! Skinny, spotty and shy, he is constantly teased by his brothers. Left to do all the housework on the night of the ball, he dreams of escape. A slightly inept, but well-meaning fairy comes to his aid and gets him off to the ball — though not quite in human form! (*flexible thinking*)

Dantzer-Rosenthal, Marya. *Some Things Are Different, Some Thing Are the Same*. Illus. by Miriam Nerlove. Whitman, 1986. (Ages 4–8).
Steven and Josh, two small boys, compare and contrast diverse aspects of their homes, their lives and their daily routines. List as many well known book characters as you can (*fluency*). Group the characters by similarities and differences. Think of as many groups as you can (*flexibility*).

Dinardo, Jeffrey. *The Wolf Who Cried Boy*. Illus. by author. Grosset, 1989. (Ages 4–8).
Young wolf likes nothing better than playing practical jokes on his neighbors. One day, turtle, pig and cat, tired of hearing the wolf cry "boy," decide to teach him a lesson. Together they climb inside of a "boy" costume and scare the wits out of the wolf, who — it can be certain — will never try that trick again (*flexible thinking*).

French, Fiona. *Snow White in New York*. Illus. by author. Oxford University Press, 1990. (Ages 6–10).
Set in New York City in the Jazz Age of the 1920s, Snow White is a beautiful jazz baby protected by seven hot jazzmen. Instead of a wicked stepmother, her arch-enemy is the Queen of the Underworld and her Prince Charming is a crack reporter from the *New York Mirror* (*flexible thinking*).

Geringer, Laura. *A Three Hat Day*. Illus. by Arnold Lobel. Harper and Row, 1985. (Ages 3–6).
On a gloomy day R.R. Pottle III wears three hats to cheer himself up. Then at the town's biggest hat store he meets Isabel, a fellow hat lover. Name as many kinds of hats as you can (*fluency*). Group the hats you named (*flexibility*). Write a non-fiction picture book showing different workers' hats and telling why they wear those hats.

Harrison, David L. *Wake Up, Sun!* Illus. by Hans Wilhelm. Random, 1986. (Ages 2–4).
A silly dog does not see the sun when he wakes up in the middle of the night. He asks for help from his thick-headed friends to find it. Think *flexibly*. How could you get the moon back if a brownie captured it and threw it in a deep lake?

Heine, Helme. *The Pigs' Wedding*. Illus. by author. McElderry, 1986. (Ages 4–8).
After sending out invitations by smoke signal, Porker and Curlytail have a wedding celebration that none of their friends will ever forget. Be *original*. Draw those foods you would expect to see at a pigs' wedding feast. Compare your ideas with those of the author/illustrator of this book.

_____. *Prince Bear*. Illus. by author. McElderry, 1990. (Ages 4–8).
Long, long ago, when fairy tales were young, every bear could change into a prince and every princess could change into a bear. To be transformed, a bear had only to kiss a princess. At once, he changed and could go to the castle and live a carefree life. If a princess was bored with always being good and polite, she could kiss the first bear she found in the forest, turn into a bear, swim and fish and eat honey. Life was simple and happy.

But then, men began to cut down the forests to build highways, and to make laws about hunting and fishing. The happy balance of life was upset with sad results (*flexibility*).

Hoban, Russell. *Monsters.* Illus. by Quentin Blake. Scholastic Hardcover, 1990. (Ages 2–4).
John likes to draw monsters. He draws monsters with hundreds of eyes and ears; he draws scaly monsters, furry monsters and unheard of monsters that are so monstrous they have to be invisible so they won't scare themselves to death. What will happen when John begins to draw the biggest monster ever? Write an *original* poem about your favorite kind of monster.

Howe, James. *There's a Monster under My Bed.* Illus. by David Rose. Atheneum, 1986. (Ages 3–6).
Simon knows there is a monster under his bed because he can hear it breathing. But when he finally gets up the courage to look he finds it is. . . . Be *fluent* . . . how many things could the monster be?

Jonas, Ann. *The Trek.* Illus. by author. Greenwillow, 1985. (Ages 3–6).
A walk to school becomes an exciting safari, as water hole, desert, river, trading post and more must be passed before the mountain (school steps) is reached. What things do you pass on the way to school? What might they remind you of? A stoplight is like an apple because. . . . A garden gate is like a _____ because. . . . Think *flexibly.*

Leaf, Margaret. *Eyes of the Dragon.* Illus. by Ed Young. Lothrop, 1987. (Ages 4–8).
An artist agrees to paint a dragon on the wall of a Chinese village, but the magistrate's insistence that he paint eyes on the dragon has amazing results. What could they possibly be? Think of many ideas. Think in *flexible* ways.

McQueen, John. *A World Full of Monsters.* Illus. by Marc Brown. Crowell, 1986. (Ages 3–6).
A look at a world of 100 years ago when monsters did all of the day-to-day jobs that humans do now. *Fluency:* How many different jobs can you name? *Flexibility:* How could you group the jobs you named?

Madsen, Ross. *Perrywinkle and the Book of Magic Spells.* Illus. by Dirk Zimmer. Dial, 1986. (Ages 4–8).
All kinds of mishaps occur when Perrywinkle takes his father's "Book of Magic Spells" to school. Students will have fun thinking of *original* spells they would like to use at school.

Marshall, James. *Goldilocks and the Three Bears.* Illus. by author. Dial, 1988. (Ages 3–6).
Papa Bear, Mama Bear and little Baby Bear were mighty hungry after their long morning ride. But when they returned to their beautiful Victorian home, it was in a terrible state. Their porridge, left cooling on the dining room table, had been eaten. Baby Bear's chair was broken into little pieces. And upstairs the intruder slept. Who wold have thought one little girl could have caused such pandemonium?
More elaboration than parody, Marshall's version is ideal for younger children but his inventive touches will be appreciated by older students as well (*elaboration*).

Martin, Rafe. *Foolish Rabbit's Big Mistake.* Illus by Ed Young. Putnam, 1985. (Ages 3–6).
  When a rabbit hears a crashing sound, he decides the earth is breaking up. As he spreads the warning the animals stampede with almost disastrous results. Be a *fluent* thinker. How many different things could cause a crashing sound in the woods?

Parish, Peggy. *Amelia Bedelia Goes Camping.* Illus. by Lynn Sweat. Greenwillow, 1985. (Ages 4–8).
  Amelia Bedelia knows there is more than one way to pitch a tent. She pitches it right into the bushes. She rows a boat by putting it in line with the other boats. *Flexible thinking* at its best! How many other tasks can you think of that might not get done if they were interpreted literally?

Ross, Tony. *Foxy Fables.* Illus. by author. Dial, 1986. (Ages 4–8).
  A retelling with a twist of six of Aesop's fables. Here is a challenge to students to do some *original* thinking. What other fables could be given a modern twist?

Rounds, Glen. *Wash Day on Noah's Ark.* Illus. by author. Holiday, 1985. (Ages 6–10).
  When the ark finally reaches land, Mrs. Noah has all of the wash to do, surrounded by fighting animals and no clothesline. Be a *flexible* thinker. If you had no clothesline and no dryer, how could you dry clothes?

Ryder, Joanne. *The Night Flight.* Illus. by Amy Schwarts. Four Winds, 1985. (Ages 4–8).
  Here is an imaginative, *original* approach to a walk in the park. While in the park Anna finds goldfish can talk, a stone lion comes to life and she can fly like a wild bird. What *original*, imaginary things might happen to you on your walk to a friend's house?

Schweninger, Ann. *Birthday Wishes.* Illus. by author. Viking Kestrel, 1986. (Ages 2–4).
  The Rabbit family comes up with tons of ideas, each better than the one before, to make Buttercup's birthday full of surprises. Guess what the ideas are before you share the book. Be *original*.

Smith, Wendy. *The Lonely, Only Mouse.* Illus. by author. Viking Kestrel, 1986. (Ages 3–6).
  Thelonius, an only mouse child *evaluates* the positive and negative aspects of being alone.

Stanley, Diane. *The Good Luck Pencil.* Illus. by Bruce Degen. Four Winds, 1986. (Ages 4–8).
  What if you had a magic pencil that could help you get perfect scores in math? What other things would you want the pencil to do? Be *fluent*. Think of many things. Now look at your list. How many of these things could you do yourself without the help of a magic pencil?

Vesey, A. *The Princess and the Frog.* Illus. by author. Atlantic Monthly Press, 1985. (Ages 4–8).
  The princess waits impatiently for the frog she brings to the palace to turn into a prince but he seems only to grow fat and bossy. A *flexible* new twist on an old tale.

Yolen, Jane. *Sleeping Ugly.* Illus. by Diane Stanley. Coward, 1981. (Ages 5–9).
  Princess Miserella is beautiful on the outside but ugly on the inside. Plain Jane is just the opposite. When a slightly muddled Good Fairy takes a hand, things get put right in a most unexpected way (*flexible thinking*).

Yorinks, Arthur. *Hey, Al.* Illus. by Richard Egielski. Farrar, 1986. (Ages 4–8).
  Al, a janitor, and Eddie, his dog, live together in a single room on the West Side until they are offered a new life in paradise by a mysterious bird. They discover, however, that paradise is not what they expected. Be *original*, create a drawing of *your* idea of what paradise would be.

10
Books Too Good to Miss!

This is not meant to be an all-inclusive list. It is a list of favorites of the author who has had success in sharing these titles with children.

Books Without Words

Alexander, Martha. *Out! Out! Out!* Dial, 1968.
Anno, Mitsumasa. *Anno's Journey.* Philomel, 1985.
Briggs, Raymond. *The Snowman.* Little, Brown, 1985.
Collington, Peter. *Little Pickle.* Dutton, 1986.
Goodall, John. *Surprise Picnic.* Holiday House, 1977.
Hutchins, Pat. *Changes, Changes.* Macmillan, 1971.
Krahn, Fernanco. *Sebastian and the Mushroom.* Delacorte, 1976.
MacGregor, Marilyn. *Baby Takes a Trip.* Four Winds, 1985.
Mayer, Mercer. *Oops!* Dial, 1977.
Sasaki, Isao. *Snow.* Viking, 1980.
Spier, Peter. *Dreams.* Doubleday, 1986.
Winter, Paula. *The Bear and the Fly.* Crown, 1976.
Young, Ed. *The Other Bone.* Harper and Row, 1984.
————. *Up a Tree.* Harper and Row, 1983.

For Toddlers

Ahlberg, Janet and Ahlberg, Allan. *Peek-a-Boo.* Viking, 1981.
Barrett, Judy. *What's Left?* Atheneum, 1983.
Brown, Marc. *Hand Rhymes.* Dutton, 1985.
Brown, Margaret Wise. *Goodnight Moon.* Harper, 1947.
Bruna, Dick. *B Is for Bear.* Methuen, 1967.
Burningham, John. *The Blanket.* Crowell, 1976.
Campbell, Rod. *Dear Zoo.* Four Winds, 1983.
Crews, Donald. *Freight Train.* Greenwillow, 1978.
de Paola, Tomie. *Tomie de Paola's Mother Goose.* Putnam, 1985.
Dreamer, Sue. *Circus Train.* Little, Brown, 1986.
Durrell, Julie. *Mouse Tails.* Crown, 1985.

Gomi, Taro. *Where's the Fish?* Morrow, 1986.
Goodall, John. *Paddy to the Rescue.* Atheneum, 1985.
Hill, Eric. *Where's Spot.* Putnam, 1980.
Hoban, Tana. *1, 2, 3.* Greenwillow, 1985.
Isadora, Rachel. *I See.* Greenwillow, 1985.
Kalan, Robert. *Jump Frog Jump.* Greenwillow, 1981.
Kunhardt, Dorothy. *Pat the Bunny.* Golden, 1962.
Omerod, Jan. *Dad's Back.* Lothrop, 1985.
Oxenbury, Helen. *The Car Trip.* Dial, 1983.
Petty, Kate. *What's That Noise?* Watts, 1986.
Tafuri, Nancy. *Have You Seen My Duckling?* Greenwillow, 1984.
Watanabe, Shigeo. *How Do I Put It On?* Philomel, 1979.
Wells, Rosemary. *Max's First Word, Max's Ride.* Dial, 1979.

For Three- to Five-Year-Olds

Alexander, Martha. *Pigs Say Oink.* Random House, 1978.
Aliki. *Go Tell Aunt Rhody.* Macmillan, 1974.
Anno, Mitsumasa. *Anno's Counting Book.* Crowell, 1977.
_____. *Anno's Counting House.* Crowell, 1982.
Bang, Mollie. *Ten, Nine, Eight.* Greenwillow, 1983.
Briggs, Raymond. *The Mother Goose Treasury.* Coward McCann, 1966.
_____. *The Snowman.* Random, 1978.
Brown, Marc. *Finger Rhymes.* Dutton, 1980.
_____. *Hand Rhymes.* Dutton, 1985.
Brown, Marcia. *All Butterflies.* Scribner, 1974.
Bruna, Dick. *The Apple.* Methuen, 1965.
_____. *The Fish.* Methuen, 1975.
Burningham, John. *Mr. Gumpy's Outing.* Holt, 1971.
Carle, Eric. *The Grouchy Ladybug.* Harper, 1977.
_____. *The Very Hungry Caterpillar.* Philomel, 1969.
Cauley, Lorinda. *Goldilocks and the Three Bears.* Putnam, 1981.
Crews, Donald. *Freight Train.* Greenwillow, 1978.
_____. *Truck.* Greenwillow, 1980.
Galdone, Paul. *The House That Jack Built.* McGraw-Hill, 1961.
_____. *The Teeny Tiny Woman.* Clarion, 1984.
Kellogg, Steven. *Chicken Little.* Morrow, 1985.
Lobel, Arnold. *Days with Frog and Toad.* Harper, 1979.
_____. *Frog and Toad All Year.* Harper, 1976.
_____. *Frog and Toad Are Friends.* Harper, 1970.
_____. *Frog and Toad Together.* Harper, 1972.
_____. *On Market Street.* Greenwillow, 1981.
McCully, Emily. *First Snow.* Harper, 1985.
Martin, Bill, Jr. *Brown Bear, Brown Bear, What Do You See?* Holt, 1983.
Minarik, Else. *It's Spring!* Illus. by Margaret Graham. Greenwillow, 1989.
Munari, Bruno. *The Birthday Present.* Philomel, 1980.
Oxenbury, Helen. *The Helen Oxenbury Nursery Story Book.* Knopf, 1985.
Potter, Beatrix. *The Tale of Peter Rabbit.* Warne, 1902.
Rice, Eve. *Benny Bakes a Cake.* Greenwillow, 1981.

_____. *Goodnight, Goodnight.* Greenwillow, 1980.

Spier, Peter. *Crash! Bang! Boom!* Doubleday, 1972.

_____. *Fast Slow, High Low.* Doubleday, 1972.

_____. *The Fox Went Out on a Chilly Night.* Doubleday, 1961.

_____. *Noah's Ark.* Doubleday, 1977.

Wood, Audrey, and Wood, Don. *The Napping House.* Harcourt, 1984.

_____. *Heckedy Peg.* Harcourt, 1988.

Wildsmith, Brian. *Brian Wildsmith's ABC.* Watts, 1963.

_____. *Brian Wildsmith's 1.2.3s.* Watts, 1965.

For Four- to Eight-Year-Olds

Aardema, Verna. *Bringing the Rain to Kapiti Plain.* Illus. by Beatriz Vidal. Dial, 1981.

_____. *Why Mosquitoes Buzz in People's Ears: A West African Tale.* Illus. by Leo and Diane Dillon. Dial, 1975.

Alexander, Martha. *Nobody Asked Me If I Wanted a Baby Sister.* Dial, 1971.

_____. *I'll Protect You from the Jungle Beasts.* Dial, 1973.

Allard, Harry. *It's So Nice to Have a Wolf Around the House.* Illus. by James Marshall. Doubleday, 1977.

_____. *Miss Nelson Is Back.* Illus. by James Marshall. Houghton Mifflin, 1982.

Allard, Harry and Marshall, James. *Miss Nelson Has a Field Day.* Illus. by James Marshall. Houghton Mifflin, 1985.

_____. *Miss Nelson Is Missing.* Illus. by James Marshall. Houghton Mifflin, 1977.

_____. *The Stupids Have a Ball.* Illus. by James Marshall. Houghton Mifflin, 1977.

Anno, Mitsumasa. *Anno's Britain.* Philomel, 1982.

_____. *Anno's Italy.* Philomel, 1980.

_____. *Anno's Journey.* Collins, 1978.

_____. *Anno's U.S.A.* Philomel, 1983.

Arnosky, Jim. *Deer at the Brook.* Lothrop, Lee and Shepard, 1986.

Aruego, José. *Look What I Can Do.* Scribner's, 1971.

Asch, Frank. *Bear's Bargain.* Prentice-Hall, 1985.

Baker, Olaf. *Where the Buffaloes Begin.* Illus. by Stephen Gammell. Warne, 1981.

Bang, Molly. *The Grey Lady and the Strawberry Snatcher.* Four Winds, 1980.

_____. *The Paper Crane.* Greenwillow, 1985.

_____. *Ten, Nine, Eight.* Greenwillow, 1983.

Barrett, Judi. *Animals Should Definitely Not Act Like People.* Illus. by Ron Barrett. Atheneum, 1980.

_____. *Animals Should Definitely Not Wear Clothing.* Illus. by Ron Barrett. Atheneum, 1970.

Baylor, Byrd. *The Best Town in the World.* Illus. by Ronald Himler. Scribner, 1983.

_____. *Everybody Needs a Rock.* Illus. by Peter Parnall. Scribner, 1974.

_____. *Hawk, I'm Your Brother.* Illus. by Peter Parnall. Scribner, 1976.

_____. *Your Own Best Secret Place.* Illus. by Peter Parnall. Scribner, 1979.

Bemelmans, Ludwig. *Madeline.* Viking, 1962 (1939).

_____. *Madeline and the Bad Hat.* Viking, 1957.

_____. *Madeline's Rescue.* Viking, 1953.

Berger, Barbara. *Grandfather Twilight.* Philomel, 1984.

Blegvad, Lenore. *Anna Banana and Me.* Illus. by Erik Blegvad. Atheneum, 1985.

Briggs, Raymond. *Jim and the Beanstalk.* Coward-McCann, 1970.

_____. *The Snowman*. Viking, 1978.

Brown, Marc. *Arthur's April Fool*. Little, Brown, 1983.

_____. *Arthur's Eyes*. Little, Brown, 1979.

_____. *Arthur's Halloween*. Little, Brown, 1983.

_____. *Arthur's Nose*. Little, Brown, 1976.

_____. *Arthur's Tooth*. Atlantic, 1985.

_____. *Arthur's Valentine*. Little Brown, 1974.

Brown, Marcia. *All Butterflies*. Scribner, 1974.

_____. *Dick Whittington and His Cat*. Scribner's, 1950.

_____. *Once a Mouse*. Scribner's, 1961.

Brown, Margaret Wise. *The Dead Bird*. Addison-Wesley, 1958.

_____. *Goodnight Moon*. Illus. by Clement Hurd. Harper and Row, 1947.

Bryan, Ashley. *The Cat's Purr*. Atheneum, 1985.

Burningham, John. *Come Away from the Water, Shirley*. Harper, 1977.

_____. *Grandpa*. Crown, 1985.

_____. *Mr. Gumpy's Motor Car*. Harper, 1976.

_____. *Mr. Gumpy's Outing.* Holt, 1971.

_____. *Would You Rather . . .* Harper, 1978.

Burton, Virginia Lee. *Katie and the Big Snow.* Houghton Mifflin, 1943.

_____. *The Little House.* Houghton Mifflin, 1942.

_____. *Mike Mulligan and His Steam Shovel.* Houghton Mifflin, 1939.

Byars, Betsy. *Go and Hush the Baby.* Illus. by Emily Arnold McCully. Viking, 1971.

Carle, Eric. *The Mixed-Up Chameleon.* 2nd ed. Harper, 1984.

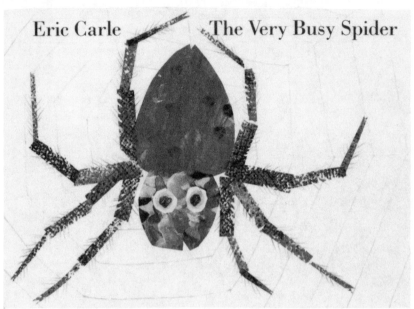

Eric Carle   The Very Busy Spider

_____. *The Very Busy Spider.* Philomel, 1984.

_____. *The Very Hungry Caterpillar.* World, 1968.

Carrick, Carol. *The Accident.* Illus. by Donald Carrick. Clarion, 1976.

_____. *The Climb.* Illus. by Donald Carrick. Clarion, 1984.

_____. *The Foundling.* Illus. by Donald Carrick. Clarion, 1977.

_____. *Lost in the Storm.* Illus. by Donald Carrick. Clarion, 1974.

_____. *Patrick's Dinosaurs.* Illus. by Donald Carrick. Clarion, 1983.

Caudill, Rebecca. *A Pocketful of Cricket.* Illus. by Evaline Ness. Holt, 1964.

Cendrars, Blaise. *Shadow.* Illus. by Marcia Brown. Scribner's, 1982.

Chaffin, Lillie. *We Be Warm Till Springtime Comes.* Illus. by Lloyd Bloom. Macmillan, 1980.

Clifton, Lucille. *Amifika.* Illus. by Thomas DiGrazia. Dutton, 1977.

_____. *The Boy Who Didn't Believe in Spring.* Illus. by Brinton Turkle. Dutton, 1973.

_____. *Everett Anderson's Friend.* Illus. by Ann Grifalconi. Holt, 1976.

_____. *Everett Anderson's Nine Month Long.* Illus. by Ann Grifalconi. Holt, Rinehart and Winston, 1978.

_____. *My Friend Jacob.* Illus. by Thomas DiGrazia. Dutton, 1980.

Cohen, Barbara. *Gooseberries to Oranges.* Illus. by Beverly Brodsky. Lothrop, Lee and Shepard, 1982.

Cohen, Miriam. *First Grade Takes a Test.* Illus. by Lillian Hoban. Greenwillow, 1980.

————. *Liar, Liar, Pants on Fire.* Illus. by Lillian Hoban. Greenwillow, 1985.

————. *Lost in the Museum.* Illus. by Lillian Hoban. Greenwillow, 1979.

Cole, Brock. *The Winter Wren.* Farrar, Straus and Giroux, 1984.

Cooney, Barbara. *Chanticleer and the Fox.* Crowell, 1958.

————. *Miss Rumphius.* Viking, 1982.

Craft, Ruth. *The Winter Bear.* Illus. by Erik Blegvad. Atheneum, 1975.

Crowe, Robert. *Clyde Monster.* Illus. by Kay Chorao. Dutton, 1976.

Dabcovich, Lydia. *Mrs. Huggins and Her Hen Hannah.* Dutton, 1985.

DeBrunhoff, Jean. *The Story of Babar.* Random House, 1960.

de Paola, Tomie. *The Cloud Book.* Holiday House, 1975.

————. *Fin M'Coul: The Giant of Knockmany Hill.* Holiday House, 1981.

————. *Helga's Dowry: A Troll Love Story.* Harcourt, 1977.

————. *Nana Upstairs, Nana Downstairs.* Penguin, 1978.

————. *Strega Nona.* Prentice-Hall, 1975.

————. *Watch Out for the Chicken-Feet in Your Soup.* Prentice-Hall, 1974.

de Regniers, Beatrice Schenk. *May I Bring a Friend?* Illus. by Beni Montresor. Atheneum, 1964.

Dragonwagon, Crescent. *Jemima Remembers.* Illus. by Troy Howell. Macmillan, 1984.

Emberley, Barbara. *Drummer Hoff.* Illus. by Ed Emberley. Prentice-Hall, 1967.

Ets, Marie Hall. *Gilberto and the Wind.* Viking, 1963.

Fair, Sylvia. *The Bedspread.* Morrow, 1982.

Fatio, Louise. *The Happy Lion.* Illus. by Roger Duvoisin. McGraw-Hill, 1954.

Feelings, Tom and Feelings, Muriel. *Jambo Means Hello: A Swahili Alphabet Book.* Dial, 1976.

————. *Moja Means One: Swahili Counting Book.* Dial, 1976.

Fisher, Aileen. *Listen Rabbit.* Illus. by Symeon Shimin. Crowell, 1964.

Freeman, Don. *Corduroy.* Viking, 1968.

————. *Dandelion.* Viking, 1964.

————. *A Pocket for Corduroy.* Viking, 1978.

Gag, Wanda. *Millions of Cats.* Coward-McCann, 1928.

————. *Nothing at All.* Coward, McCann and Geoghegan, 1941.

Gage, Wilson, *Cully Cully and the Bear.* Illus. by James Stevenson, Greenwillow, 1983.

Galdone, Joanna. *The Tailypo.* Illus. by Paul Galdone. Houghton Mifflin, 1977.

Galdone, Paul. *King of the Cats.* Houghton Mifflin, Clarion, 1985.

————. *The Three Sillies.* Houghton Mifflin, Clarion, 1981.

Galloz, Christopher, and Innocenti, Roberto. *Rose Blanche.* Illus. by Roberto Innocenti. Creative Education, 1985.

Ginsburg, Mirra. *The Chick and the Duckling.* Illus. by Jose Aruego and Ariane Aruego. Macmillan, 1972.

Goble, Paul. *The Girl Who Loved Wild Horses.* Bradbury, 1978.

————. *Star Boy.* Bradbury, 1983.

Goodall, John. *The Story of a Castle.* Atheneum, McElderry, 1986.

————. *The Story of an English Village.* Atheneum, 1979.

Gramatky, Hardie. *Little Toot.* Putnam, 1939.

Greenfield, Eloise. *She Come Bringing Me That Little Baby Girl.* Illus. by John Steptoe. Lippincott, 1974.

Hader, Berta and Hader, Elmer. *The Big Snow.* Macmillan, 1948.

Hale, Sara Josepha. *Mary Had a Little Lamb.* Illus. by Tomie de Paola. Holiday, 1984.

Haley, Gail E. *A Story, a Story.* Atheneum, 1970.

Heine, Helme. *Friends.* Atheneum, 1982.

_____. *The Most Wonderful Egg in the World.* Atheneum, 1983.

_____. *The Pigs' Wedding.* Atheneum, 1979.

Hill, Donna. *Ms. Glee Was Waiting.* Illus. by Diane Dowson. Atheneum, 1978.

Hoban, Russell. *A Baby Sister for Frances.* Illus. by Lillian Hoban. Harper, 1964.

_____. *A Bargain for Frances.* Illus. by Lillian Hoban. Harper, 1970.

_____. *Best Friends for Frances.* Illus. by Lillian Hoban. Harper, 1969.

_____. *A Birthday for Frances.* Illus. by Lillian Hoban. Harper, 1968.

Hoban, Tana. *Big Ones, Little Ones.* Greenwillow, 1976.

_____. *Of Colors and Things.* Greenwillow, 1989.

_____. *Take Another Look.* Greenwillow, 1981.

Hodges, Margaret. *Saint George and the Dragon.* Illus. by Trina Schart Hyman. Little, Brown, 1984.

Hogrogian, Nonny. *One Fine Day.* Macmillan, 1971.

Horwitz, Elinor Lander. *When the Sky Is Like Lace.* Illus. by Barbara Cooney. Lippincott, 1975.

Howard, Jane R. *When I'm Sleepy.* Illus. by Lynne Cherry. Dutton, 1985.

Hughes, Shirley. *David and Dog.* Lothrop, 1981.

Hutchins, Pat. *Don't Forget the Bacon.* Greenwillow, 1976.

_____. *The Doorbell Rang.* Greenwillow, 1986.

_____. *Good-Night, Owl!* Macmillan, 1972.

_____. *Rosie's Walk.* Macmillan, 1968.

_____. *Titch.* Macmillan, 1971.

_____. *The Very Worst Monster.* Greenwillow, 1985.

Hyman, Trina Schart. *Little Red Riding Hood.* Holiday House, 1983.

Isadora, Rachel. *Ben's Trumpet.* Greenwillow, 1979.

_____. *Max.* Macmillan, 1976.

Johnson, Tony. *The Quilt Story.* Illus. by Tomie de Paola. Putnam, 1985.

Jonas, Ann. *The Quilt.* Greenwillow, 1984.

_____. *Round Trip.* Greenwillow, 1983.

_____. *The Trek.* Greenwillow, 1985.

Joyce, William. *George Shrinks.* Harper, 1985.

Kahl, Virginia. *The Duchess Bakes a Cake.* Scribner's, 1955.

Kantrowitz, Mildred. *Maxie.* Illus. by Emily A. McCully. *Parents*, 1970.

Keats, Ezra Jack. *Dreams.* Macmillan, 1974.

_____. *Goggles.* Macmillan, 1969.

_____. *Hi Cat!* Macmillan, 1970.

_____. *A Letter to Amy.* Harper, 1968.

_____. *Louis.* Greenwillow, 1983 (1975).

_____. *Pet Show!* Macmillan, 1972.

_____. *Peter's Chair.* Harper, 1967.

_____. *The Snowy Day.* Viking, 1962.

_____. *Whistle for Willie.* Viking, 1964.

Keeping, Charles. *Joseph's Yard.* Oxford, 1969.

Kellogg, Steven. *Can I Keep Him?* Dial, 1971.

_____. *Chicken Little.* Morrow, 1985.

_____. *The Island of the Skog.* Dial, 1973.

_____. *The Mysterious Tadpole.* Dial, 1977.

————. *Pinkerton, Behave!* Dial, 1979.

————. *Ralph's Secret Weapon.* Dial, 1983.

————. *A Rose for Pinkerton.* Dial, 1981.

Kraus, Robert. *Leo the Late Bloomer.* Illus. by Jose Aruego. Crowell, 1971.

————. *Milton the Early Riser.* Illus. by Jose Aruego and Ariane Aruego. Windmill, 1972.

————. *Owliver.* Illus. by Jose Aruego and Ariane Dewey. Windmill, 1974.

Krauss, Ruth. *A Hole Is to Dig.* Illus. by Maurice Sendak. Harper, 1952.

Langstaff, John and Rojankovsky, Feodor. *Frog Went a-Courtin'.* Illus. by Feodor Rojankovsky. Harcourt, 1955.

Leaf, Munro. *The Story of Ferdinand.* Illus. by Robert Lawson. Viking, 1936.

Lexau, Joan. *Benjie on His Own.* Illus. by Don Bolognese. Dial, 1970.

————. *Emily and the Klunky Baby and the Next-Door Dog.* Illus. by Martha Alexander. Dial, 1972.

Lionni, Leo. *Alexander and the Wind-Up Mouse.* Pantheon, 1969.

————. *Fish Is Fish.* Pantheon, 1970.

————. *Frederick.* Pantheon, 1967.

————. *Inch by Inch.* Astor-Honor, 1960.

————. *Swimmy.* Pantheon, 1963.

Lobel, Arnold. *Giant John.* Harper and Row, 1964.

McCloskey, Robert. *Blueberries for Sal.* Viking, 1963.

————. *Burt Dow, Deep-Water Man.* Viking, 1963.

————. *Make Way for Ducklings.* Viking, 1963.

————. *Time for Wonder.* Viking, 1957.

McDermott, Gerald. *Arrow to the Sun: A Pueblo Indian Tale.* Viking, 1974.

McPhail, David. *The Bear's Toothache.* Little, Brown, 1972.

————. *Fix-It.* Dutton, 1984.

————. *Pig Pig Goes to Camp.* Dutton, 1983.

Mahy, Margaret. *Jam: A True Story.* Illus. by Helen Craig. Little, Brown, 1986.

Marshall, James. *George and Martha.* Houghton Mifflin, 1972.

————. *George and Martha Tons of Fun.* Houghton Mifflin, 1972.

Martin, Bill, Jr., and Archambault, John. *The Ghost-Eye Tree.* Illus. by Ted Rand. Holt, Rinehart and Winston, 1985.

————. *White Dynamite and Curly Kid.* Illus. by Ted Rand. Holt, Rinehart and Winston, 1986.

Maruki, Toshi. *Hiroshima No Pika.* Lothrop, 1980.

Mathis, Sharon Bell. *The Hundred Penny Box.* Illus. by Leo and Diane Dillon. Viking, 1975.

Mayer, Mercer. *There's a Nightmare in My Closet.* Dial, 1968.

Miles, Miska. *Annie and the Old One.* Illus. by Peter Parnall. Little, Brown, 1971.

Milne, A.A. *The House at Pooh Corner.* Illus. by Ernest H. Shepard. Dutton, 1928.

Mosel, Arlene. *The Funny Little Woman.* Illus. by Blair Lent. Dutton, 1972.

Ness, Evaline. *Sam, Bangs and Moonshine.* Holt, 1966.

Noble, Trinka H. *The Day Jimmy's Boa Ate the Wash.* Illus. by Steven Kellogg. Dial, 1980.

Parish, Peggy. *Amelia Bedelia.* Illus. by Fritz Siebel. Harper and Row, 1963.

Perrault, Charles. *Cinderella.* Illus. by Marcia Brown. Scribner, 1954.

Piper, Watty. *The Little Engine That Could.* Illus. by George Hauman and Doris Hauman. Platt and Munk, 1954 (1930).

Politi, Leo. *The Nicest Gift.* Scribner, 1973.

————. *Song of the Swallows.* Scribner, 1949.

Potter, Beatrix. *Mrs. Tittlemouse and Other Mouse Stories.* Warne, 1985.
_____. *The Tale of Benjamin Bunny.* Warne, 1904.
_____. *The Tale of Jemima Puddle Duck.* Warne, 1908.
Provensen, Alice and Provensen, Martin. *The Glorious Flight Across the Channel with Louis Bleriot.* Viking, 1983.
Quackenbush, Robert. *First Grade Jitters.* Lippincott, 1982.
Rayner, Mary. *Garth Pig and the Ice Cream Lady.* Atheneum, 1977.
_____. *Mr. and Mrs. Pig's Evening Out.* Atheneum, 1976.
Rey, H.A. *Curious George.* Houghton Mifflin, 1941.
Robbins, Ruth. *Baboushka and the Three Kings.* Illus. by Nicolas Sidjakov. Parnassus, 1960.
Ryan, Cheli Duran. *Hildilid's Night.* Illus. by Arnold Lobel. Macmillan, 1971.
Rylant, Cynthia. *Miss Maggie.* Illus. by Thomas DeGrazia. Dutton, 1983.
_____. *The Relatives Came.* Illus. by Stephen Gammel. Bradbury, 1985.
_____. *When I Was Young in the Mountains.* Illus. by Diane Goode. Dutton, 1982.
Sendak, Maurice. *In the Night Kitchen.* Harper, 1970.
_____. *Where the Wild Things Are.* Harper, 1963.
Seuss, Dr. pseud. (Theodor S. Geisel). *And to Think That I Saw It on Mulberry Street.* Vanguard, 1937.
_____. *The Cat in the Hat.* Random, 1957.
_____. *Horton Hatches the Egg.* Random, 1940.
_____. *The Lorax.* Random, 1971.
_____. *McElligot's Pool.* Random, 1947.
_____. *Scrambled Eggs Super.* Random, 1953.
Sharmat, Marjorie Weinman. *Attilla the Angry.* Illus. by Lillian Hoban. Holiday House, 1985.
_____. *Gila Monsters Meet You at the Airport.* Illus. by Byron Barton. Macmillan, 1980.
_____. *I'm Terrific.* Illus. by Kay Chorao. Holiday House, 1977.
Shulevitz, Uri. *Dawn.* Farrar, Straus and Giroux, 1974.
_____. *One Monday Morning.* Scribner's, 1976.
_____. *Rain Rain Rivers.* Farrar, Straus and Giroux, 1969.
Slobodkina, Esphyr. *Caps for Sale.* W.R. Scott, 1947.
Spier, Peter. *Bored! Nothing to Do!* Doubleday, 1978.
_____. *London Bridge Is Falling Down.* Doubleday, 1967.
_____. *Noah's Ark.* Doubleday, 1977.
_____. *Peter Spier's Rain.* Doubleday, 1982.
Stanley, Diane. *A Country Tale.* Four Winds, 1985.
Stanovich, Betty Jo. *Big Boy, Little Boy.* Illus. by Virginia Wright-Frierson. Lothrop, 1984.
Steig, William. *Abel's Island.* Farrar, Straus and Giroux, 1976.
_____. *The Amazing Bone.* Farrar, Straus and Giroux, 1976.
_____. *Amos and Boris.* Farrar, Straus and Giroux, 1971.
_____. *Doctor DeSoto.* Farrar, Straus and Giroux, 1982.
_____. *Sylvester and the Magic Pebble.* Windmill, 1979.
Stevenson, James. *Could Be Worse!* Greenwillow, 1977.
_____. *Oh No, It's Waylon's Birthday!* Greenwillow, 1989.
_____. *That Terrible Halloween Night.* Greenwillow, 1980.
_____. *What's Under My Bed?* Greenwillow, 1983.
Testa, Fulvio. *If You Take a Pencil. . . .* Dial, 1982.
Tresselt, Alvin. *Hide and Seek Fog.* Illus. by Roger Duvoisin. Lothrop, 1965.

_____. *White Snow, Bright Snow.* Illus. by Roger Duvoisin, Lothrop, 1947.

Udry, Janice May. *Let's Be Enemies.* Illus. by Maurice Sendak. Harper and Row, 1959.

_____. *The Moon Jumpers.* Illus. by Maurice Sendak. Harper, 1959.

_____. *A Tree Is Nice.* Illus. by Marc Simont. Harper, 1956.

Ungerer, Tomi. *The Beast of Monsieur Racine.* Farrar, Straus and Giroux, 1971.

_____. *Zeralda's Ogre.* Harper, 1967.

Van Allsburg, Chris. *The Garden of Abdul Gasazi.* Houghton Mifflin, 1979.

_____. *Jumanji.* Houghton Mifflin, 1981.

_____. *The Mysteries of Harris Burdick.* Houghton Mifflin, 1984.

Vincent, Gabrielle. *Ernest and Celestine's Picnic.* Greenwillow, 1982.

_____. *Smile, Ernest and Celestine.* Greenwillow, 1982.

Viorst, Judith. *Alexander and the Terrible, Horrible, No Good, Very Bad Day.* Illus. by Ray Cruz. Atheneum, 1972.

_____. *Alexander Who Used to Be Rich Last Sunday.* Illus. by Ray Cruz. Atheneum, 1978.

_____. *I'll Fix Anthony.* Illus. by Arnold Lobel, Harper, 1969.

_____. *The Tenth Good Thing About Barney.* Illus. by Erik Blegvad. Atheneum, 1971.

Waber, Bernard. *The House on East 88th Street.* Houghton Mifflin, 1962.

_____. *Ira Sleeps Over.* Houghton Mifflin, 1972.

Wagner, Jenny. *John Brown, Rose and the Midnight Cat.* Illus. by Ron Brooks. Bradbury, 1978.

Walter, Mildred Pitts. *My Mama Needs Me.* Illus. by Pat Cummings. Lothrop, 1983.

Ward, Lynd. *The Biggest Bear.* Houghton Mifflin, 1952.

Wells, Rosemary. *Benjamin and Tulip.* Doubleday, 1973.

_____. *Noisy Nora.* Dial, 1973.

Willard, Nancy. *A Visit to William Blake's Inn.* Illus. by Alice and Martin Provensen. Harcourt, 1981.

Williams, Barbara. *Albert's Toothache.* Illus. by Kay Chorao. Dutton, 1974.

_____. *Jeremy Isn't Hungry.* Illus. by Martha Alexander. Dutton, 1978.

_____. *Kevin's Grandma.* Illus. by Kay Chorao. Dutton, 1975.

Williams, Margery. *The Velveteen Rabbit.* Illus. by William Nicholson. Doubleday, 1958 (1922). Illus. by Alan Atkinson, Knopf, 1983. Illus. by Michael Hague. Holt, 1983. Illus. by Ilse Plume. Godine, 1983.

Williams, Vera B. *A Chair for My Mother.* Greenwillow, 1982.

_____. *Music, Music for Everyone.* Greenwillow, 1984.

_____. *Something Special for Me.* Greenwillow, 1983.

Wolff, Ashley. *The Bells of London.* Dodd, Mead, 1985.

Wood, Audrey. *King Bidgood's in the Bathtub.* Illus. by Don Wood. Harcourt Brace Jovanovich, 1985.

_____. *The Napping House.* Illus. by Don Wood. Harcourt, 1984.

Yashima, Taro. pseud. (Aun Iwamatsu). *Crow Boy.* Viking, 1955.

Zemach, Margot. *Hush, Little Baby.* Dutton, 1976.

Zion, Gene. *Harry, the Dirty Dog.* Illus. by Margaret Bloy Graham. Harper, 1956.

Zolotow, Charlotte. *Do You Know What I'll Do?* Illus. by Garth Williams. Harper, 1958.

_____. *If It Weren't for You.* Illus. by Ben Shecter. Harper, 1966.

_____. *Mr. Rabbit and the Lovely Present.* Illus. by Maurice Sendak. Harper, 1962.

_____. *The Storm Book.* Illus. by Margaret Bloy Graham. Harper, 1952.

Number and Math Concepts

Addition

Allen, Pamela. *Who Sank the Boat.* Coward, 1983.
Anno, Mitsumasa. *Anno's Counting House.* Philomel, 1982.
Bright, Robert. *Mi Paragua Roja.* Morrow, 1968.
————. *My Red Umbrella.* Morrow, 1985.
Carle, Eric. *Rooster Is Off to See the World.* Studio, USA, 1987.
Seuss. Dr. *Five Hundred Hats of Bartholomew Cubbins.* Hale, 1938.
Tresselt, Alvin. *The Mitten.* Lothrop, 1964.

Counting Stories

Anno, Mitsumasa. *Anno's Counting Book.* Crowell, 1975.
Argent, Kerry and Trinca, Rod. *One Woolly Wombat.* Kane Miller Bk., 1985.
Blegvad, Lenore. *One Is for the Sun.* Harcourt, 1968.
Boynton, Sandra. *Hippos Go Berserk.* Little, 1986.
Bright, Robert. *Mi Paragua Roja.* Morrow, 1968.
Carle, Eric. *1, 2, 3, to the Zoo.* World, 1968.
Charles, Donald. *Cuenta con Gato Galano.* Children's, 1984.
Crews, Donald. *Ten Black Dots.* Greenwillow, 1986.
de Regniers, Beatrice Schenk. *So Many Cats.* Illus. by Ellen Weiss. Clarion, 1985.
Feelings, Muriel. *Moja Means One: Swahili Counting Book.* Illus. by Tom Feelings.
    Dial, 1971.
Friskey, Margaret. *Pollito Pequenito Cuenta Hasta Diez.* Children's, 1984.
Gretz, Susanna. *Teddy Bears 1 to 10.* Four Winds, 1978.
Hoban, Tana. *Count and See.* Macmillan, 1978.
Hutchins, Pat. *One Hunter.* Greenwillow, 1981.
Inkpen, Mick. *One Bear at Bedtime.* Little, 1988.
Kitamura, Satoshi. *When Sheep Cannot Sleep.* Farrar, Straus and Giroux, 1986.
Kitchen, Bert. *Animal Numbers.* Dial, 1987.
Langstaff, John and Rojankovsky, Feodor. *Over in the Meadow.* HBJ, 1973.
Lindbergh, Reeve. *The Midnight Farm.* Dial, 1987.
McDonald, Suse. *Numblers.* Dial, 1988.
Macmillan, Bruce. *Counting Wildflowers.* Lothrop, 1986.
Peavy, Paul. *One Dragon's Dream.* Bradbury, 1978.
Sendak, Maurice. *One Was Johnny.* Harper, 1962.
Tafuri. Nancy. *Have You Seen My Duckling?* Greenwillow, 1984.
Wildsmith, Brian. *Brian Wildsmith's 1, 2, 3's.* Watts, 1965.
Zaslansky, Claudia. *Count on Your Fingers African Style.* Crowell, 1980.

Division

Hutchins, Pat. *The Doorbell Rang.* Greenwillow, 1986.
Slobodkina, Esphyr. *Caps for Sale.* Scott, 1940.

Fractions

Emberley, Ed. *Ed Emberley's Picture Pie*. Little, 1984.
Lionni, Leo. *Pezzettino*. Pantheon, 1975.
Mathews, Louise. *Gator Pie*. Illus. by Jeni Bassett. Dodd, 1979.
Silverstein, Shel. *Missing Piece*. Harper, 1976.

Large Numbers

Barrett, Judith. *Benjamin's 365 Birthdays*. Macmillan, 1978.
Gag, Wanda. *Millions of Cats*. Coward, 1928.
Modell, Frank. *One Zillion Valentines*. Greenwillow, 1981.
Schwartz, David. *How Much Is a Million?* Illus. by Steven Kellogg. Lothrop, 1986.
Seuss, Dr. *The Five Hundred Hats of Bartholomew Cubbins*. Hale, 1938.
Sharmat, Majorie Weinman. *The Three Hundred Twenty-Ninth Friend*. Illus. by Cyndy
   Szekeres. Four Winds, 1979.

Logic

Birch, David. *The King's Chessboard*. Dial, 1988.
Burns, Marilyn. *The Book of Think*. Little, 1976.
Nozaki, Akihiro. *Anno's Hat Tricks*. Illus. by Mitsumasa Anno. Philomel, 1985.
Shannon, George. *Stories to Solve: Folktales from Around the World*. Greenwillow,
   1985.
Vernon, Adele. *The Riddle*. Dodd, 1987.
Vivelo, Jackie. *Beagle in Trouble: Super Sleuth II*. Putnam, 1986.

Measurement

Carle, Eric. *Will You Be My Friend?* Crowell, 1971.
Dobrin, Arnold. *Peter Rabbit's Natural Food Cookbook*. Warne, 1977.
Lionni, Leo. *Inch by Inch*. Astor-Honor, 1960.
MacGregor, Carol. *The Fairy Tale Cookbook*. Macmillan, 1983.

Money

Heide, Florence. *Treehorn's Treasure*. Holiday, 1981.
Hoban, Tana. *26 Letters and 99 Cents*. Greenwillow, 1987.
Merrill, Jean. *The Toothpaste Millionaire*. Houghton, 1974.
Shook Hazen, Barbara. *Tight Times*. Illus. by Trina Schart Hyman. Viking, 1979.
Viorst, Judith. *Alexander Who Used to Be Rich Last Sunday*. Illus. by Ray Cruz.
   Atheneum, 1978.
Williams, Vera. *A Chair for My Mother*. Greenwillow, 1982.

Multiplication

Anderson, Lonzo. *Two Hundred Rabbits.* Viking, 1972.
Anno, Masaichiro and Anno, Mitsumasa. *Anno's Mysterious Multiplying Jar.* Illus. by Mitsumasa Anno. Philomel, 1983.
Emberley, Ed and Emberley, Barbara. *One Wide River to Cross.* Prentice, 1966.
Mathews, Louise. *Bunches and Bunches of Bunnies.* Illus. by Jeni Bassett. Dodd, 1978.
Yoeman, John. *Sixes and Sevens.* Macmillan, 1971.

Optical Illusions

Anno, Mitsumasa. *Anno's Alphabet: An Adventure in Imagination.* Crowell, 1975.
———. *Topsy Turvy.* Walker-Weatherhill, 1970.
Baun, Arline and Baun, Joseph. *Opt: An Illusionary Tale.* Viking, 1978.
Jonas, Ann. *Round Trip.* Greenwillow, 1983.
Simon, Seymour. *The Optical Illusion Book.* Morrow, 1976.

Ordinal Numbers

Becker, John. *Seven Little Rabbits.* Scholastic, 1985.
Cleveland, David. *The April Rabbits.* Illus. by Nurit Karlin. Coward, 1978.
Langstaff, John and Rojankovsky, Feodor. *Frog Went A-Courting.* HBJ, 1955.
McDermott, Gerald. *Anansi the Spider.* Holt, 1972.
Martin, Bill. *Monday, Monday, I Like Monday.* Holt, 1970.
———. *Ten Little Squirrels.* Holt, 1970.

Shapes

Emberley, Ed. *Ed Emberley's Picture Pie.* Little, 1984.
———. *The Wings on a Flea.* Little, 1961.
Fisher, Leonard. *Look Around, a Book About Shapes.* Viking, 1987.
Hoban, Tana. *Circles, Triangles and Squares.* Macmillan, 1974.
———. *Shapes, Shapes, Shapes.* Greenwillow, 1986.
Hutchins, Pat. *Changes, Changes.* Macmillan, 1971.
Kessler. *Are You Square?* Doubleday, 1966.
Reiss. *Shapes.* Bradbury, 1974.
Wildsmith, Brian. *Brian Wildsmith's Puzzles.* Watts, 1970.

Size

Brenner, Barbara. *Mr. Tall and Mr. Small.* Addison, 1966.
Brett, Jan. *Goldilocks and the Three Bears.* Illus. by author. Dodd, 1987.
Carle, Eric. *The Grouchy Ladybug.* Crowell, 1977.
———. *Will You Be My Friend?* Crowell, 1971.
Hoban, Tana. *Is It Larger? Is It Smaller?* Greenwillow, 1985.
Kalan, Robert. *Blue Sea.* Illus. by Donald Crews. Greenwillow, 1979.
Krauss, Ruth. *Big and Little.* Scholastic, 1987.

Lionni, Leo. *The Biggest House in the World.* Pantheon, 1968.
Titherington, Jeanne. *Big World, Small World.* Greenwillow, 1985.

Subtraction

Bang, Molly. *Ten, Nine, Eight.* Greenwillow, 1983.
Barrett, Judi. *What's Left.* Atheneum, 1983.
Duncan, Joyce. *A Cake for Barney.* Orchard, 1988.
Mack, Stan. *Ten Bears in My Bed.* Pantheon, 1974.
Mathews, Louise. *The Great Take-Away.* Illus. by Jeni Bassett. Dodd, 1980.
Sendak, Maurice. *One Was Johnny.* Harper, 1962.
Warren, Cathy. *Ten Alarm Camp Out.* Lothrop, 1983.

Time

Anno, Mitsumasa, et al. *All in a Day.* Philomel, 1986.
Carle, Eric. *The Grouchy Ladybug.* Crowell, 1977.
_____. *The Very Hungry Caterpillar.* Putnam, 1981.
Clifton, Lucille. *Everett Anderson's Year.* Holt, 1974.
Coats, Laura Jane. *The Oak Tree.* Macmillan, 1987.
Gibbons, Gail. *The Seasons of Arnold's Apple Tree.* HBJ, 1984.
Hutchins, Pat. *Clocks and More Clocks.* Macmillan, 1970.
Martin, Bill. *Monday, Monday, I Like Monday.* Holt, 1970.
Provensen, Alice and Provensen, Martin. *The Year at Maple Hill Farm.* Macmillan, 1978.
Sendak, Maurice. *Chicken Soup with Rice.* Harper, 1962.
Viorst, Judith. *Sunday Morning.* Illus. by Hilary Knight. Macmillan, 1968.

Weight

Johnston, Tony. *Farmer Mack Measures His Pig.* Illus. by Megan Lloyd. Harper, 1986.
Lexau, Joan. *Archimedes Takes a Bath.* Crowell, 1969.

Appendix
Ages and Stages!

Books to Meet the Needs of Young Children as They Grow and Develop Mentally

	Characteristics	Look for Books That	Examples
Ages 1 and 2	• Uses all five senses to discover the world. • Learns by doing. • Uses language to name things.	• Have repeating sounds. • Involve the child. • Bring words and objects together.	*Mother Goose* *I Hear, I See, I Touch* Rachel Isadora. *Peek-a-Boo* Janet and Allan Ahlberg.
Ages 2 to 4	• Learns by experience. • Egocentric. • Rapid language development. • Likes routine. • Begins to understand the idea of story.	• Deal with the world of the young child. • Have patterned and repeating language. • Have easy, short plots.	*The Story of Chicken Little* Jan Ormerod. *Max's Bath, Max's Bedtime, Max's Toys* Rosemary Wells.
Ages 4 to 6	• Uses imagination with ease. • Begins to relate to others. • More careful observer. • Sees things as good or bad. • Sense of story.	• Plots that are easy to predict. • Childhood fears dealt with positively. • Good prevails over evil. • Interesting details.	*Mr. Grumpy's Outing* John Burningham. *Millions of Cats* Wanda Gag. *Little Bear* Else Minarik.

131

Index to Authors and Titles

6500